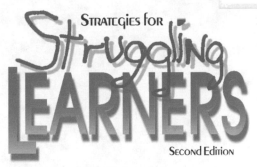

Strategies for

Struggling

LEARNERS

Second Edition

A Guide for the Teaching Parent

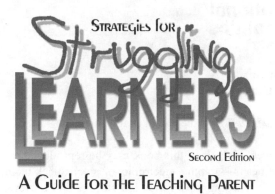

Strategies for

Struggling

LEARNERS

Second Edition

A Guide for the Teaching Parent

Joe P. Sutton, Ph.D.
Connie J. Sutton, M.A.Ed.

Exceptional Diagnostics

220 Douglas Drive • Simpsonville, SC 29681

Exceptional Diagnostics

220 Douglas Drive
Simpsonville, SC 29681

Cover Design: Brian Johnson, Samuel Laterza
Typesetting: Samuel Laterza, Richard Bowers
Production Manager: Larry Goodwin
Printer: Electric City Printing, Inc.
Cover Photography: Unusual Films

Library of Congress Catalog Card Number: 97-60456

Recommended Cataloging in Publication Data

Sutton, Joe P. (Joe Perry), 1956-
    Strategies for struggling learners: a guide for the
    teaching parent / Joe P. Sutton, Connie J. Sutton
    –2nd ed.
    p. cm.
    Included bibliographical references and index.
    ISBN 0-9645684-1-1
    1. Special education—United States. 2. Home
    schooling. I. Sutton, Connie J.,1956-   . II. Title
                1997
    371.9'26—dc20   97-60456
                                       CIP

Printed in the United States of America
10 9 8 7 6 5 4 3 2 1

Dedication

To our sons, Jeremy, Jason, Jared, who patiently endured
while Mom and Dad struggled to write this book.
We will always love you.

Table of Contents

Preface

In order to get help for their struggling learners, parents traditionally have had to lean largely on learning specialists in conventional schools or therapists in clinical settings, sometimes both. Unfortunately, experts continue to fuel a sense of helplessness and dependence among parents. According to Beechick,[1] some professionals arrogantly contend that "parents can't be expected to know" how to help their own children. They believe that the parents' role, if any, is subservient to their own in educating struggling learners. Moreover, these same professionals maintain that, without their direct intervention, struggling learners can never be effectively educated.

We are reminded of a mother in Idaho who, prior to home schooling, decided to observe her son's special education teacher at the nearby public school. Displeased with a number of things she saw (the classroom was an absolute circus!), the mother confronted the teacher. Embarrassed at her own incompetence, yet intent on reasserting her control, the teacher pompously said to the mother, "We hope that in time you will trust us for what is best for your child."

We reject the view that conventional educators and other professionals are the only ones who can effectively teach struggling learners, that they know what is best, and that parents essentially can do little or nothing to help. To the contrary we believe that parents, of all people, know what is best for their children. More important, we believe that parents are quite capable of teaching their own children, regardless of limitations in learning, attention, or behavior that the children may have. Furthermore, parents don't need professional credentials in special education or psychology in order to be effective. We concur with Mrs. Melbar, a home school mother from Texas, who has passionately argued, "What qualifications do I have to teach [my] disabled child? None, other than the fact that I am his mother."[2]

Now in its second edition, this book, presented in ten chapters, seeks to provide parents with strategies (i.e., "plans of action") that will better equip them to meet the educational needs of their own children at home. In Chapter 1, we discuss *Learners with Limitations* and provide a brief overview of the more prevalent disabilities found among school-age children today. Chapter 2 helps parents establish a

Framework for Teaching that finds its roots in five basic Scriptural principles and follows the model of the Master Teacher, Christ Jesus. We devote Chapter 3 to a discussion of the essentials of *Testing and Evaluation* that apply to children with disabilities and others who struggle.

In Chapter 4, we present two major approaches to *Developing Curriculum* for struggling learners. Parents learn how to tailor-make an educational program, understand the difference between remediation and regular instruction, and grasp the concept of an individualized educational plan (IEP). Chapter 5 on *Program Practices* provides parents with helpful suggestions on how to set up a daily teaching schedule, compile a permanent folder, secure consulting services, and more.

Chapter 6 focuses on *Modifying Instruction*. Included are suggestions on how parents can adapt their teacher behaviors, instructional processes, and the learning environment. We introduce *Generic Teaching Methods* in Chapter 7 that can be used to teach just about any subject. Methods for *Teaching the 3 R's* are provided in Chapter 8, specifically those found to be more effective in teaching reading, spelling, and mathematics to struggling learners. Ideas for *Teaching Study Skills* such as outlining, memorization, and time management are provided in Chapter 9. Finally, Chapter 10 describes numerous techniques for *Managing Behavior*, which parents may need to implement in order to make learning more efficient.

We would be amiss if we failed to recognize the following individuals who graciously served as original reviewers of our book: Tom and Sherry Bushnell, National Challenged Homeschoolers Associated Network; Inge Cannon, executive director, Education PLUS®; Sharon Grimes, national convention speaker; Dr. Carl Herbster, president, American Association of Christian Schools; and Scott W. Somerville, Esq., attorney, Home School Legal Defense Association. Their wise counsel and helpful suggestions were invaluable.

The Lord has truly been our Strength in completing this second edition. By His grace, we have not wavered in our mission to provide parents with a reliable resource on how to teach struggling learners more effectively in the home. Our prayer is that parents will faithfully implement these *Strategies for Struggling Learners*, and that they will receive encouragement from these pages to keep on keeping on.

JPS & CJS

---

[1]Beechick, R. (1991), p. 49.
[2]Melbar, G. (1990), p. 54.

Strategies for

Struggling

LEARNERS

Second Edition

A Guide for the Teaching Parent

1

Learners with Limitations

Perfection. Only the Lord Jesus Himself has experienced perfection on this side of eternity. All other men and women since the beginning of time have lived with limitations of some kind. What a dismally bleak future it would be if there were no hope of a perfect existence to come. But we know that the redeemed in Christ will be perfect one day, for the Scripture promises that "we shall all be changed" (I Cor. 15:51), and "we shall be like Him" (I John 3:2). As wonderful as these truths are, we will nonetheless have to endure the limitations the Lord places upon us while we remain in this world.

The limitations that most people may bear will be little more than the usual basic aches, pains, and worries that every man and woman has experienced since Adam's fall. But for some, limitations may involve diminished abilities and skills. For example, some people have great difficulty communicating publicly and cringe at the thought of having to speak before an audience of more than two or three other people. Yet these same individuals are generally able to express themselves effectively on a one-to-one basis. Others have two "left feet" and lack the agility necessary to participate, even leisurely, in sports and athletic activities. Yet these same people are quite capable of walking and getting around in a day-to-day, routine way.

Still for others, God allows more severe limitations, typically referred to as *disabilities*, which may significantly impair their learning, behavior, emotional and/or physical capabilities. Students with disabilities can be found in almost any educational setting—public, Christian, and home schools alike. What many parents may not realize, though, is just how many disabled students there really are.

According to the U.S. Department of Education,[1] approximately 4.8 million children (or about 10% of the school age population) were classified as disabled and served in public school special education classrooms during the 1990-91 school year. One may wonder whether this figure holds true for students in the home school population. Unfortunately, there are no reliable, published figures on the numbers of students with disabilities in home schools. Nonetheless, Janet (Wayne) Walker,[2] has estimated that approximately 5% of the home school population of students have disabilities. She bases this figure on information about children with disabilities supplied by the parents who hold membership with the Home School Legal Defense Association (HSLDA).

Interestingly, Wayne's figure coincides with the percentage of students with documented disabilities found in private Christian schools, which is between 4.8% and 5.5%.[3] We believe that this figure is probably not reflective of the *true* number of children with disabilities in Christian schools, however, and that the actual figure is much closer to that reported above for public schools. Since Christian schools for the most part (94%) do not have formal special education programs, it may well be that there are many students sitting in regular classrooms who have legitimate disabilities, but have not been referred, evaluated, and identified properly.

We believe the situation is similar in home schools across America. Since home education includes much individualized instruction, some parents may already be modifying and accommodating instruction for children who, in reality, differ significantly from the norm in learning, attention, and behavior, and would likely be classified as disabled if evaluated.

In short, we simply cannot deny the significant numbers of students with disabilities and their need for tailor-made instruction. Moreover, we cannot be so shortsighted as to think that students with disabilities will only be found in public or private schools. God is no respecter of persons (Acts 10:34), and students with disabilities will be found in home schools, too. Parents who are part of the burgeoning home education movement in America must recognize students with disabilities for the unique creation that they are (Ps. 139:14). An important first step that must precede developing tailor-made programs of home instruction is understanding characteristics and behaviors of the various exceptionalities, one or more of which *may* be at the root of a child's learning struggles.

Forms of Exceptionality

Drs. Hallahan and Kauffman,[4] two leading special education scholars, identify and describe eight major forms of exceptionality that children may have:

- emotional-behavior disorders;
- hearing impairments;
- giftedness;
- mental retardation;
- learning disabilities;
- physical-health impairments;
- speech-language disorders; and
- visual impairments.

The most prevalent disability reported by the U.S. Department of Education[5] is learning disability, which represents almost half (49.1%) of all children with disabilities. Speech-language disorders comprise approximately one fourth (22.7%) of the entire group. Students with mental retardation (12.7%) and emotional-behavior disorders (9%) represent another sizeable proportion of the disabled school population.

Interestingly, although the remaining disabilities have received considerably more media hype and attention that the other disabilities mentioned above, they represent a very small percentage of the total number of students with disabilities. These include physical-health impairments (2.4%), multiple disabilities (2.2%), hearing impairments (1.4%), and visual impairments (.5%). Unfortunately, federal officials do not include figures on gifted and talented students in their annual report to Congress, but the Office of Gifted and Talented in Washington has traditionally held that about 3% to 5% of the school population is gifted.[6]

Disabilities range from mild to severe in the degree that they may affect a child's ability to succeed academically, vocationally, socially, and/or behaviorally. What follows is a brief description of each disability. For additional reading, we refer our readers to a more comprehensive discussion of disabilities in a book entitled, *Special Education: A Biblical Approach.*[7] See Appendix A for information on how to secure this book.

Learning Disabilities

The term *learning disability* was coined by Dr. Sam Kirk in the early 1960's and officially defined by Congress in Public Law 94-142 in 1975. Prior to this time, many terms were used to describe this unique group of children including *minimal brain injury, cerebral dysfunction, central nervous system disorder, conceptually handicapped, perceptually handicapped,* and *educationally handicapped,* to name a few.

While other disabilities such as retardation and blindness have been recognized for centuries, learning disability (not just learning problems) has only recently been acknowledged as a bona fide disability. Nonetheless there have doubtless been individuals with learning disabilities since the beginning of time. Historical evidence suggests that a number of important and famous people through the ages have had learning disabilities including Nelson Rockefeller, Thomas Edison, August Rodin, Woodrow Wilson, and Albert Einstein. More recently, the actor, Henry Winkler (who played the *Fonz* on the television sitcom, *Happy Days*), was identified as learning disabled during his grade school years.

Describing a learning disability (LD) can be difficult, since "symptoms are not the same from person to person."[8] That is, not all LD students demonstrate the same array of characteristic behaviors. What we do know for sure, though, is that the characteristics of LD students are numerous and varied. After analyzing a large group of LD students from across the country, Clements[9] reported the following ten most frequently found symptoms: hyperactivity, perceptual-motor problems, general coordination problems, emotional lability (frequent mood shifts), attention disorders, impulsivity, memory/thinking deficits, specific academic problems, speech/language/hearing problems, and neurological irregularities (abnormalities in brain activity). Learning disabled students may also demonstrate difficulties in information processing, learning strategy acquisition and usage, motivation, and social skills.[10,11]

The definition of specific learning disabilities adopted by the federal government in Public Law 94-142 and reiterated more recently in Public Law 101-476 (Individuals with Disabilities Education Act) has been the most commonly accepted standard for identifying learning disabled students.[12] The definition is lengthy, laboriously worded, and even ambiguous in places, but from it we can glean five key criteria.

1. Normal/above normal intelligence. The first distinguishing characteristic of learning disabled students is that their intelligence scores generally fall within the normal range, that is, between 85 and 115.[13] It is clear that normal to above normal intelligence sets students with true learning disabilities apart from other students who have learning difficulties which may be stemming from subaverage, low intelligence. For example, students with mental retardation also have severe learning difficulties, but mentally retarded students by definition have intelligence quotients (IQ's) that are below 70 to 75.

2. Underachievement in one or more academic areas. In addition to normal to above normal intelligence, students with learning disabilities also demonstrate severe underachievement in one or more *academic* areas. In fact, academic problems are the most prominent, identifying characteristic of learning disabled students. Hallahan and Kauffman contend that, "by definition, if there is no academic problem, a learning disability does not exist."[14] The federal definition states that a child may have a specific learning disability in one or more of the following language arts, and/or mathematics related areas: (1) basic reading skills; (2) reading comprehension; (3) written expression (including spelling); (4) listening comprehension; (5) oral expression; (6) mathematics calculation; and (7) mathematics reasoning.

3. Discrepancy between intelligence and achievement. The identifying criterion contained in federal law that is least disputed by scholars is establishment of "a severe discrepancy between [the child's] achievement and intellectual ability."[15] One's intellectual ability is simply one's God-given ability to think, reason, remember, process information, acquire knowledge, and learn. Intelligence, then, is a reflection of a child's *potential* or capability to learn. Achievement, on the other hand, is a reflection of what a child has *actually* learned and is typically measured through paper and pencil type tests.

Herein lies the great paradox with learning disabled children. Their normal to above normal intelligence suggests that they *should* be able to demonstrate better than average mastery of academic work (i.e., A's and B's for those who grade conventionally) with little or no struggle. But in reality, they experience continual learning difficulties, severe at times, and at best earn only average (i.e., C's) and below average (i.e., D's), even failing grades (i.e., F's) at times. When parents have these children evaluated by professionals, their resulting achievement scores are very low. To establish a severe discrepancy, examiners must prove that there is a mismatch or gap between the child's potential to learn (i.e., his intellectual ability), measured by individual intelligence tests, and his actual learning and performance (i.e., his achievement), measured by one-on-one achievement tests. This generally requires the use of statistical analyses.

4. Psychological processing problems. A fourth identifying criterion is that LD students will show psychological processing problems. This simply means that the child will have difficulty with input and output of information during instruction and other times. The end result is that the student will not efficiently and accurately produce the desired response (i.e., writing, speaking, pointing, moving, etc.). Some students have problems processing visual information, while others have problems processing auditory information. Some may have problems in both areas.

Conventional school teachers generally vouch that LD students have processing problems, for it can be detected quite easily when these students are required to take notes in class. The act of notetaking calls for the student to process visual and/or auditory information the teacher presents. He must then quickly paraphrase the information while it is in his short-term memory and reproduce it in written form in his notebook. Parents may see similar difficulties in the home when they ask these children to complete errands requiring multiple steps (e.g., "Go to your room, pick up your dirty clothes, put your toys away,..."). Unfortunately, many parents view the child's failure to comply with commands as deliberate disobedience, when, in fact, the problem may be reflective of a processing weakness.

5. Difficulties not due to other factors. Finally, the federal definition of learning disability makes it clear that a bona fide learning disability will be a distinct condition. The term *learning disability* does not apply to "children who have learning problems which are primarily the result of visual, hearing, or motor handicaps, of mental retardation, of emotional disturbance, or of environmental, cultural, or economic disadvantage..."[16] Simply put, a true learning disability will not be the *primary result* of any other existing limitation, although a learning disability may exist concomitantly with another disability such as attention deficit disorder or emotional-behavior disorder.

We regret that some diagnosticians today do not follow the federal definition for learning disability. It is not unusual to hear of a child who has been labeled as *visually learning disabled*, *learning disabled in memory*, or *learning disabled in attention*. Informed parents will immediately recognize that these are not true learning disabilities, for visual, memory, and attention problems are not academic problems per se, but problems of a sensory-perceptual or cognitive nature. Moreover, these so-called learning disabilities are simply not recognized under the federal definition of learning disabilities. When professionals do not follow proper identifying criteria as they should, they may classify students as learning disabled who really are not (which results in overidentification) or they may fail to label those students who actually have a true learning disability (which results in underidentification).

One term that has survived the years that is used synonymously with learning disabilities is *dyslexia*, although it is becoming increasingly outdated. Dyslexia was a term coined in the early years of the special education movement in America and reflected a more medical, neurological orientation. The problem with using this term is that we cannot document neurological dysfunction in most learning disabled students, although we do presume it. Only in some severely learning disabled students can neurological dysfunction be proven. People today who embrace the term *dyslexia* will nonetheless attest to the same typical reading decoding (i.e., pronunciation) and reading comprehension problems[17] in these children that are described under the federal definition of learning disability in reading.

Parents should recognize the magnitude of the numbers of children nationwide who have learning disabilities. The likelihood of having a child with a learning disability is far greater than that of any other disability. As we mentioned earlier, almost half of all students identified as disabled are learning disabled. In comparison to other forms of disability, we now know that learning disabled students outnumber visually impaired students 98 to 1, hearing impaired students 35 to 1, students with multiple forms of disability 22 to 1, physically impaired students 20 to 1, emotional-behavior disordered students 5 to 1, mentally retarded students 4 to 1, and speech-language disordered students 2 to 1.[18]

Speech-Language Disorders

Speech-language disorders (also referred to as *communication disorders*) represent some of the most disheartening of all disabilities. Imagine a child who is trying to communicate something to his parent or teacher, perhaps a need, and cannot because of a speech or language limitation. Children with communication disorders have just as much need for special education as those children with specific learning disabilities, mental retardation, or other disability, if their limitation adversely affects their academic work.

Communication disorders include serious problems in speech and/or language. A speech disorder means that the student has significant deficiencies in his ability to deliver and intelligibly transmit a message to listeners. Language disorders, on the other hand, have to do with the actual message itself, not the mechanics of delivering the message. A child's inability to choose words carefully and to structure these words appropriately in sentences so that the intended meaning is conveyed to the listener is the essence of a language disorder.

Speech disorders occur in three specific subtypes: (1) articulation; (2) voice; and (3) fluency problems. Speech disorders of articulation are by far the most prevalent. Approximately three-fourths of all speech disordered children have problems in articulation. Examples of articulation problems include substitutions (e.g., "wabbit" for rabbit), additions (e.g., "idear" for idea), omissions (e.g., "baball" for baseball), and distortions (e.g., "ax" for ask).

Some children have voice speech disorders, which would include significant problems in voice quality (e.g., mellow, thin, hyponasal, or rough sounding voices), pitch (e.g., monotone voices), and magnitude of sound (e.g., voices that arc either too loud or too soft). Finally, some students will have speech disorders in fluency (called *dysfluencies*), stuttering being the most common type.[19]

Children with language disorders may show significant problems in the use of phonemes (word sounds without meaning such as "ch"), morphemes (word sounds with meaning such as "*in*-ability"), syntax (rules of grammar and word usage), semantics (word meanings and relationships among words), and/or pragmatics (social use of language). Speech and language disorders are formally diagnosed by a speech-language pathologist.

Mental Retardation

Students with mental retardation (sometimes referred to as *mental disability* or *developmental disability*) share some of the same behavioral characteristics as students with learning disabilities, including problems with attention, memory, organizing information, misbehavior (e.g., disruptiveness, distractibility), motivation, oral language, academic underachievement (especially reading), social skills (including self-esteem problems), emotional reactions and responses, and overall delayed development.[20,21]

Students classified as mentally retarded must meet three conditions: (1) subaverage intellectual functioning; (2) severe maladaptive behavior skills; and (3) manifestation of the condition between birth and 18 years of age. Subaverage intellectual functioning simply means that the child has an intelligence quotient (IQ) that is well below normal. Luckasson and his colleagues[22] have indicated that the American Association on Mental Retardation now requires that a student's IQ must fall below 70 to 75 (average IQ ranges from 85 to 115) in order to qualify for classification as mentally retarded.

Adaptive behavior skills are "composed of a number of coping skills that, when combined, allow an individual to achieve community integration."[23] Children who are truly mentally retarded will have great difficulty in this area. Examples of adaptive behavior skills would include independent functioning (e.g., eating, dressing, toilet use), physical development (sensory and motor), economic activity (e.g., money and shopping skills), language development, numbers and time skills, prevocational/vocational activities, self-direction (e.g., initiative, perseverance, leisure time), responsibility, and so on. Depending on the degree of subaverage intellectual functioning and severity of maladaptive behavior skills, students with mental retardation have traditionally been classified as mild (formerly *educable*), moderate (formerly *trainable*), or severe/profound in their condition.

Emotional-Behavior Disorders

Students with emotional-behavior disorders, along with those classified as learning disabled or mentally disabled, are referred to as *mildly disabled*.[24,25] The U.S. Department of Education[26] has indicated that approximately 75% of all disabled students in this country have mild conditions of disability.

Emotional-behavior disorders are the most difficult forms of disability to diagnose in children. Hallahan and Kauffman report that much subjectivity is presently involved in identifying these students since "no one has come up with an objective standard that is understandable and acceptable."[27] Nonetheless it is generally agreed that emotional-behavior disordered students will exhibit behaviors that are *extremely different* (not just somewhat different), *chronic* (i.e., not short-lived), and *unacceptable* (when viewed in light of social or cultural expectations).

Emotional-behavior disordered students typically have low-average intelligence and may show academic deficits in their school work (generally one or more years below their assigned grade level). In addition, their characteristic behaviors may include hyperactivity, distractibility, impulsivity, overt aggression (e.g., arguing, cruelty, fighting, disobedience, threatening), covert antisocial acts (e.g., truancy, negativism, poor peer associations, destructiveness), anxiety-withdrawal (e.g., fearfulness, feelings of inferiority, oversensitivity), depression, and/or general unhappiness.[28,29]

In most Christian circles today, people continue to grapple with the legitimacy of disabilities in general. Many simply don't believe that disabilities are real, despite the clear examples of disabilities in Scripture.[30] However, based on Biblical evidences of disabilities, our extensive study of research of the more prevalent disabilities, and our personal experiences in teaching children with disabilities, we are confident that all of the disabilities discussed in this chapter should be accepted without question as bona fide, God-allowed conditions, except for one—emotional-behavior disorders.

Our view is that many, if not most, of the students identified in public schools as emotional-behavior disordered are simply not disabled at all. Rather they are suffering from what every human has since Adam, and that is *spiritual impairment*. Their actions and attitudes prior to emitting many of their inappropriate behaviors are more reflective of intentional disobedience and defiance of authority (secular educators call it *noncompliance*), which, more accurately, are behaviors that emanate from unrighteous, sinful hearts. In short, they have sin natures that have been allowed to run out of control by parents and school officials. We find it interesting that Kauffman[31] identifies research which has concluded that certain temperaments in children, if left unharnessed and unmanaged (i.e., undisciplined), could develop into so-called behavior disorders.

We do believe that there are some genuine cases of emotional-behavior disorders in children, albeit very few. We have personally read evaluation reports of students who have biologically-based, chemical imbalances which produce extreme, chronic, and totally unacceptable behavior in Christian contexts. But these cases are rare. We believe that, in order to prove the legitimacy of an emotional-behavior disorder, the following additional requirements must be satisfied as part of a full, comprehensive psychoeducational evaluation (see Chapter 3) of the child:

- Evidence of significantly low ratings on at least two different behavior rating scales;
- Verification of behavior problems through at least three classroom observations (randomly selected times) over an extended time period and in different settings (e.g., playing with others, during class time, etc.);
- Interviews with parents and teachers to determine whether the student's poor behavior is extreme, chronic, and unacceptable based on Christian culture expectations;
- Determination of whether the child's behavior is due to intentional, overt disobedience, incompetence (i.e., insufficient or no instruction in how to behave correctly), or test-based long-term memory deficits; and

- Evidence of a physiological, biological, biochemical, and/or neurological basis for the problem behaviors (which would require substantiation through a neurological examination—e.g. electroencephalogram, etc.).

Physical-Health Impairments

Although students with physical-health impairments represent only a very small proportion (about 5 in every 100 disabled children) of the disabled population of school-age children, a myriad of conditions fall under this category. Examples include cancer, hemophilia, diabetes, sickle cell anemia, clubfeet, and even AIDS. By definition, physically impaired students are those whose

physical limitations or health problems interfere with school attendance or learning to such an extent that special service, training, equipment, materials, or facilities are required...[and] whose *primary* characteristics are [not] visual or auditory impairments.[32]

It is important to note, however, that physically impaired students may have visual or hearing problems that are secondary to their primary physical limitation. In addition, these students may also have "mental retardation, emotional disturbance, speech and language disorders, or special gifts or talents"[33] that co-exist with their physically disabling conditions.

Neurologically-based physical impairments would include such conditions as cerebral palsy, epilepsy (seizure disorders), spina bifida, poliomyelitis, and multiple sclerosis. There are also physical impairments of the *musculoskeletal* type, such as muscular dystrophy and arthritis. Other causes of physical impairment include *congenital malformations* (of the heart, hip, legs, arms, head, and/or face), *accidents* (e.g., burning, poisoning, bike/car mishaps), *child abuse* (e.g., physical, mental, sexual abuse), and *child neglect* (e.g., nutritional neglect).[34] Children are generally classified as physically impaired by medical doctors.

Attention Deficit Disorder

Identification criteria for attention deficit/hyperactivity disorder (the more common term is *attention deficit disorder* or ADD) are not delineated in federal law. In fact, prior to the early 1990's, students with ADD were not even considered eligible for special education services in the public schools unless they were concurrently classified with one or more of the traditionally recognized forms of disability such as learning disability, speech-language disorders, mental retardation, emotional-behavior disorder, etc.

In 1991, however, the U.S. Department of Education essentially recognized ADD as a disability by ruling that ADD children may now receive special education under the label of *other health impairment* if school officials determine that their condition is a "chronic or acute health problem that results in limited alertness, which adversely affects educational performance."[35] When the 3% to 5% of ADD students are factored in, the overall prevalence of students with disabilities in this country has the potential to soar to about 15%.

Some people mistakenly refer to ADD as a type of LD; but ADD is *not* a form of learning disability or vice versa. There are clear distinctions between the two conditions. While a learning disability has to do with academic problems per se, the primary focus of ADD is three other domains of behavior—inattention, hyperactivity, and impulsivity.[36] It is not unusual, though, for ADD students to experience learning *difficulties*. We have noted earlier in this chapter that inattention is one of the top ten characteristic symptoms of LD students.

Not all ADD children exhibit behavior problems in all three areas of inattention, hyperactivity, and impulsivity. Some will show behavior problems predominately in inattention, while others have difficulties primarily in hyperactivity and impulsivity. Some of the effects of ADD, however, are the same in most of these students, regardless of the different combinations of behaviors. For example, their academic school work many times is below average, and their organizational skills and interactions with friends are less than desirable.[37] Like LD students, ADD students will have *normal intelli-*

gence for the most part,[38] which sets them apart from students who may have severe attention and behavioral problems that result primarily from other disabilities such as mental retardation.

Interestingly, all children will exhibit some problems in inattention, hyperactivity, or impulsivity at one time or another in their lives. But true ADD students will emit one or more of these behaviors at intense levels, not just a little, and in numerous, very specific ways, not just in a general way. Moreover, in its 1994 fourth edition of the *Diagnostic and Statistical Manual of Mental Disorders,*[39] the American Psychiatric Association (APA) has stipulated that other conditions must occur in conjunction with emitted behaviors in order for a student to qualify for classification as ADD. According to the APA, an ADD student may have one of the following three subtypes:

- **Attention-Deficit/Hyperactivity Disorder, Predominantly Inattentive Type.** This subtype should be used if six (or more) symptoms of inattention (but fewer than six symptoms of hyperactivity-impulsivity) have persisted for at least 6 months.[40]

Inattention

(a) often fails to give close attention to details or makes careless mistakes in schoolwork, work, or other activities

(b) often has difficulty sustaining attention in tasks or play activities

(c) often does not seem to listen when spoken to directly

(d) often does not follow through on instructions and fails to finish schoolwork, chores, or duties in the workplace (not due to oppositional behavior or failure to understand instructions)

(e) often has difficulty organizing tasks and activities

(f) often avoids, dislikes, or is reluctant to engage in tasks that require sustained mental effort (such as schoolwork or homework)

(g) often loses things necessary for tasks or activities (e.g. toys, school assignments, pencils, books, or tools)

(h) is often easily distracted by extraneous stimuli

(i) is often forgetful in daily activities[41]

- **Attention-Deficit/Hyperactivity Disorder, Predominantly Hyperactive-Impulsive Type.** This subtype should be used if six (or more) symptoms of hyperactivity-impulsivity (but fewer than six symptoms of inattention) have persisted for at least 6 months.[42]

Hyperactivity

(a) often fidgets with hands or feet or squirms in seat
(b) often leaves seat in classroom or in other situations in which remaining seated is expected
(c) often runs about or climbs excessively in situations in which it is inappropriate (in adolescents or adults, may be limited to subjective feelings of restlessness)
(d) often has difficulty playing or engaging in leisure activities quietly
(e) is often "on the go" or often acts as if "driven by a motor"
(f) often talks excessively[43]

Impulsivity

(g) often blurts out answers before questions have been completed
(h) often has difficulty awaiting turn
(i) often interrupts or intrudes on others (e.g., butts into conversations or games)[44]

- **Attention-Deficit/Hyperactivity Disorder, Combined Type.** This subtype should be used if six (or more) symptoms of inattention and six (or more) symptoms of hyperactivity-impulsivity have persisted for at least 6 months.[45]

The diagnostician will also be looking at other factors before recommending final classification of ADD. For example, a determination has to be made as to whether:

- the behaviors are being demonstrated "to a degree that is maladaptive and inconsistent with [the] developmental level"[46] of average children of the same chronological age;
- some behaviors "were present before age 7 years";[47]
- the symptomatic behaviors "[are] present in two or more settings (e.g., at school [or work] and at home)";[48]

- the ADD condition significantly impairs the child's social, academic, or occupational functioning;[49] and
- "The symptoms do not occur exclusively..." as part of or "are not better accounted for" by other selected mental disorders (e.g., anxiety disorder, etc.).[50]

While ADD and LD each are separate and distinct conditions, there is evidence to suggest that ADD and LD can co-exist in children. That is, a child can meet all minimal criteria for *both* conditions at the same point in time. There are situations, then, when a diagnostician may determine that the child's attention and learning difficulties are not due primarily to either of the two conditions alone, but may be stemming from both conditions. Fowler[51] has reported that approximately 25% of children with ADD also have a concurrent form of LD. In their analysis of other research studies, J. W. Lerner and her colleagues[52] concluded that estimates of the coexistence of ADD and LD range from 9% to 63%.

Hearing Impairments

Students who are deaf or hearing impaired can be born with the condition (congenital) or may acquire it sometime after birth (adventitious). One classification system is based on the amount of hearing loss, typically measured in decibels by an audiologist. Decibel units are a measure of intensity or loudness of sound. With the use of a pure tone audiometer, an audiologist will determine the student's threshold (beginning or onset) for hearing sound. Students with normal hearing should be able to hear sounds slightly above 0 decibels (db). Those with a hearing loss will only be able to hear sounds at decibel levels of greater magnitude and are classified with varying levels of hearing loss as follows: 26-54 db (mild); 55-69 db (moderate); 70-89 (severe); and 90 db and above (profound).[53]

Another system of classification for students with hearing impairment is more educational in nature. School officials who will be providing special education for these children are more concerned with the extent to which hearing loss affects the development and use of language. Under this system, *deaf* students are those who cannot process language through their hearing sense, even with the use of hearing devices. Those who can successfully process language with or without hearing devices are considered *hearing impaired*.[54]

The intellectual ability of hearing impaired students has been a point of considerable controversy among experts for some time now.[55] Since intelligence testing has traditionally relied upon intact hearing ability and spoken language processing skills, those with hearing impairment have tended to earn lower intelligence scores on these tests. It is now believed, however, that if these students are administered tests via manual communication (e.g., sign language), their intelligence scores would not fall in the retardation range.[56]

Visual Impairments

A visual impairment, like a hearing impairment, is a sensory disability and not a cognitive or academic form of disability, although both a visual and a hearing impairment can adversely affect a child's learning and achievement. Visual impairments can be defined from both legal and educational perspectives.

The legal classification system is based on *visual acuity* (how clearly one can see) and *field of vision* (i e , one's peripheral vision) skills. According to Hallahan and Kauffman, a legally blind person has "visual acuity of 20/200 or less in the better eye even with correction (e.g., eyeglasses) or has a field of vision so narrow that its widest diameter subtends an angular distance no greater than 20 degrees."[57] A person who is legally partially blind/sighted will have a visual acuity between 20/70 and 20/200 in the better eye with corrective lenses. One should interpret a visual acuity level such as "20/70" to mean that the visually impaired student can see at 20 feet what a normally-sighted person can see at 70 feet.

The educational definition of visual impairment is based on the child's mode of reading instruction. If the child's vision is so impaired that he cannot read print and must use Braille or audiotapes/records in order to learn to read, then he is considered *blind*. *Low vision* students, on the other hand, are visually impaired students who can read print, but must have the print enlarged through magnification or large-print books (or copier enlargements).

Human nature as it is, some people may doubt the intellectual capabilities of visually impaired students. They surmise that if a student is not created perfectly whole then he cannot think, reason, and learn satisfactorily. But like students with hearing impairment, "there is no reason to believe that blindness results in lower intelligence."[58]

Giftedness

Giftedness is an exceptionality that is different from other disabilities in that it is a *positive* condition that we want to foster in a child, not eliminate or eradicate. Gifted students generally do not have academic deficits that need remediation per se; rather, they have an abundance of certain skills and talents that should be encouraged. Unlike students with learning disabilities, attention deficit disorders, or mental retardation, a gifted student's exceptionality is not preventing him from achieving or performing at acceptable levels. To the contrary, he comes into a typical learning situation many times having already mastered in whole or in part the skill or task that is being taught. We agree with Colangelo and Davis that "an inadequate and unchallenging curriculum...can extinguish the high potential accomplishment of gifted children and adolescents."[59] Like students with disabilities, then, gifted students still need special education that meets their unique needs. For the most part, appropriate educational programming will include either accelerated instruction, enrichment instruction, or a combination of both.

Traditionally, the label of *gifted and talented* has been reserved for those students who score unusually high on intelligence tests. This somewhat limited and narrow, single-criterion definition for giftedness has presented problems for educators through the years. Surely, our readers have known people who showed unusually brilliant intelligence and were considered gifted, but simply could not demonstrate or manifest their giftedness through some "remarkable or valued contribution to the human condition."[60] Yet there have been other students with only high average intelligence (and, hence, not considered gifted) who nonetheless demonstrated their unusual talent by excelling in some performance or skill area (e.g., music, athletics, etc.).

The U.S. Department of Education defines gifted students as

...[those] who by virtue of outstanding abilities, are capable of high performance. Children capable of high performance include those with demonstrated achievement and/or potential ability in any of the following areas singly or in combination: 1. general intellectual ability; 2. specific academic aptitude; 3. creative or productive thinking; 4. leadership ability; 5. visual and performing arts; 6. psychomotor ability.[61]

Renzulli, Reis, and Smith[62] suggested a new definition for giftedness that includes three criteria. (1) *high ability* (may include elevated intelligence), (2) *high creativity*, and (3) *high task commitment*. However, Renzulli and Reis have indicated that, "it is not necessary for a student to possess all three characteristics..." and that gifted students only have to "display or have the potential to display above-average ability in one or more academic areas, or in special aptitudes such as music, art, drama, leadership, or interpersonal skills."[63] While the remaining two characteristics (i.e., high creativity and high task commitment) are considered developmental objectives,[64] an individual will manifest his giftedness when he "applies [all three characteristics] to performance in a specific endeavor."[65]

Specific performance areas for giftedness are numerous and might include cartooning, poetry, costume design, architecture, cooking, agriculture, and many others. We must move away from the typical misconception that gifted students are only the "bookworms" in our classrooms. A truly gifted student can be one whose area of talent and excellence falls outside the boundaries of paper-and-pencil tests or straight-A's on a report card.

---

[1] U.S. Department of Education (1992)
[2] J. Sutton, Wayne, Lanier, & Salars (1993)
[3] J. Sutton, Everett, & C. Sutton (1993)
[4] Hallahan & Kauffman (1991)
[5] U.S. Department of Education (1992)
[6] Wolf (1994)
[7] J. Sutton (1993c)
[8] Beechick (1993), p. 45
[9] Clements (1966)
[10] Hallahan & Kauffman (1991)
[11] Lerner (1989)
[12] Hallahan & Kauffman (1991)
[13] Hallahan & Kauffman (1991)
[14] Hallahan & Kauffman (1991)
[15] *Federal Register*, December 19, 1977, p. 65083.
[16] *Federal Register*, December 19, 1977, p. 65093.
[17] Williams (1988)
[18] U.S. Department of Education (1992)
[19] Hallahan & Kauffman (1991)
[20] Hallahan & Kauffman (1991)
[21] Patton, Bierne-Smith, & Payne (1990)
[22] Luckasson, Coulter, Polloway, Reiss, Schalock, Snell, Spitalnick, & Stark (1992)
[23] Lambert, Nihira, & Leland (1993), p. 2
[24] Houck & McKenzie (1988)

[25]Kelly & Vergason (1991)
[26]U.S. Department of Education (1986)
[27]Hallahan & Kauffman (1991), p. 174
[28]Hallahan & Kauffman (1991)
[29]Kauffman (1989)
[30]J. Sutton (1990)
[31]Kauffman (1989)
[32]Hallahan & Kauffman (1991), p. 344
[33]Hallahan & Kauffman (1991), p. 344
[34]Hallahan & Kauffman (1991)
[35]U.S. Department of Education (1991), p. 3
[36]J. Sutton (1996)
[37]J. Sutton (1994d)
[38]Kauffman (1989)
[39]American Psychiatric Association (1994)
[40]DSM-IV, p. 80
[41]DSM-IV, p. 83-84
[42]DSM-IV, p. 80
[43]DSM-IV, p. 84
[44]DSM-IV, p. 84
[45]DSM-IV, p. 80
[46]DSM-IV, p. 83, 84
[47]DSM-IV, p. 84
[48]DSM-IV, p. 84
[49]DSM-IV, p. 84
[50]DSM-IV, p. 85
[51]cited in J. W. Lerner, Lowenthal, & S. R. Lerner (1995)
[52]J. W. Lerner, Lowenthal, & S. R. Lerner (1995)
[53]Hallahan & Kauffman (1991)
[54]Brill, Macneil, & Newman (1986)
[55]Hallahan & Kauffman (1991)
[56]Sullivan (1982)
[57]Hallahan & Kauffman (1991), p. 304
[58]Hallahan & Kauffman (1991), p. 302
[59]Colangelo & Davis (1991), p. 4
[60]Hallahan & Kauffman (1991), p. 405
[61]Marland (1972), p. 5.
[62]Renzulli, Reis, & Smith (1981)
[63]Renzulli & Reis (1991), p. 114
[64]Renzulli & Reis (1991)
[65]Hallahan & Kauffman (1991), p. 406

2

Framework for Teaching

Y our framework for teaching is much like the foundation of
a building. How meticulously contractors construct the
foundation of a building, yet they are sometimes lax in finishing other
aspects of the structure, for example, the dry walling or painting.
Rarely, though, are they careless in the foundation of the building.
Why? Given human nature and the depravity of man, contractors
may be more concerned for the moment about meeting required building codes! But beyond this, we know that the foundation must be
carefully constructed, using the best materials, because the contin-
ued strength and longevity of the building and its ability to withstand
time and the environment depends largely on the stability of the foundation.

So it is with a framework for teaching. Core teaching beliefs
and values are the infrastructure to well-designed educational programs. Every instructional decision made about children from choice
of curricula, to teaching methods and materials, even expectations of
success conveyed to them through the years are impacted by the teaching beliefs and values embraced by their parents. In order for Christian parents to teach struggling learners effectively, their framework
for teaching must reflect a Christian philosophy.

But what does philosophy mean? Of the eleven definitions[1] for *philosophy*, three have particular relevance for the teaching parent: (a) fundamental beliefs; (b) motivating concepts and principles; and (c) values. In short, a parent's philosophy are her beliefs about teaching.

One of the basic requirements in teaching struggling learners effectively in the home, as we shall discuss more fully in the chapters to come, is individualizing and tailor-making their instruction, which is what conventional educators typically refer to as *special education*. It would be easy, then, for parents to simply adopt the philosophy of special education embraced by public educators, and be done with it. But we agree with Vaughn, who cautions that, in formulating a *Christian* philosophy of special education, one must be careful not to "Christianize...secular special education philosophy."[2]

What Christian parents believe about their children who struggle with regard to who they are and how they should be taught runs counter to much of what secular educators believe. One public school special education teacher interviewed for an television documentary[3] articulated seven goals for her students with learning disabilities. She wanted them to (1) be literate; (2) be functional; (3) be self-supportive; (4) acquire skills necessary for life; (5) get a good job; (6) feel good about oneself; (7) be confident; and (8) be one person not on welfare. We would certainly agree that these goals are good from the perspective that they foster development of a child into adulthood. However, taken collectively, these goals tend to reflect virtual self-sufficiency, which runs counter to dependence upon God. Moreover, her list of goals is absent of any godly virtues.

Herein lies one of the major philosophical problems that we have with the secular special education movement in America. From the outset, it is clear that early proponents pushed for public school special education programs, but did so with essentially a self-centered, self-serving mission in mind. They argued simply that students with disabilities had a right to a free, appropriate public education. Christian parents will immediately recognize that, as the Lord's people, none of us really have any rights per se. All we have is granted to us by the grace and goodness of God. Even the salvation we have is not a right; rather, it is a gift, a privilege from a merciful, loving God (John 3:16).

While we agree that all struggling learners, particularly those with disabilities, should have an appropriate education that is designed to meet their unique needs, we disagree with some of the militant, civil rights approaches and initiatives that preceded the passage of federal laws which mandated special education in American public schools in the 1970's. Therefore, we believe parents of struggling learners should reject any Christianized approach to secular special education. A more appropriate framework for teaching should stem directly from God's Holy, infallible Word. We believe that a proper framework, then, will center on the following: (1) integrating basic teaching principles; and (2) emulating the Master Teacher.

Integrating Teaching Principles

The five basic, Scriptural teaching principles that follow are ones we believe are most important for parents who have struggling learners with bona fide disabilities. There are other Bible truths and principles that we could include, but the five we identify below are most essential. Parents who have nondisabled struggling learners should also consider these five principles carefully, for these Biblical truths are applicable to their home education efforts, too.

These five teaching principles can be deceptively simple. At first glance, one could conclude that they are a bit elementary. While this may be true to some extent, in a day and age where truth is constantly attacked, challenged, and distorted by liberal unbelievers, it is important that we acknowledge and reaffirm these basic, godly teaching principles as the basis for teaching struggling learners in the home.

Principle 1

Students with disabilities have a sin nature and will sin. Unlike Rousseau, the great philosopher-teacher of centuries past who believed that all children were inherently good, God's Word is unmistakenly clear that all men (and students) are sinners. There is simply nothing good in man. One doesn't have to read too far into the Scripture to realize just how sinful man really is. In the book of Genesis (3:1-6), God tells us that man fell into sin. We learn in Psalm 51:5 that man was born into sin. Numerous passages in the New Testament teach that mankind continues to inherit a sinful nature (Romans 3:9-12; Romans 5:12; I Cor. 15:21-22).

Accepting this principle as truth is not difficult for most Christian parents who have nondisabled children, particularly when they see their children in selfish moments. Some parents who have a child with a disability, though, may find it very hard to accept the fact that their child with all his limitations and afflictions also has a weakness with sin. Perhaps they rationalize that the disability in and of itself is enough for the child to bear, and that a loving, benevolent God would not require the child to bear a sin nature, too. It would be very easy to excuse away a disabled child's sin nature, but to do so would be a denial of the truth. There is no exception to Romans 3:23 that "...all have sinned and come short of the glory of God." All children, disabled and nondisabled alike, have a sin nature and will sin.

No doubt parents may come to a point where they have difficulty discerning whether a particular unacceptable behavior is emanating from the child's God-given disability or from his sin nature. Only the Lord will be able to provide the wisdom necessary to discern the difference when those times come. What is unfortunate is that some sincere and well-meaning, but ignorant people automatically assume that rebellion, laziness, character flaws and the like are the sole basis for *all* learning and behavior problems. Although this may be true for many nondisabled children who misbehave and fail in their school work, we cannot accept this explanation for *all* learning and behavior problems of children with disabilities. Parents of disabled children must accept the fact that some troublesome behaviors are indeed by-products of the child's God-given disability, exercise reasonable patience and tolerance, and make every attempt over time to correct these behaviors with the Lord's help.

Principle 2

A student's disability is not necessarily a reflection of God's judgment on sin. There is a tendency many times in Christian circles to attribute a person's misfortune automatically to God's judgment on some prior sin that the person has committed. Someone suffers a heart attack or has terminal cancer, and the first thought that comes to some Christians' minds is that the person has been involved in some gross sin and that God is judging the sin through sickness.

Some even believe this to be the reason why students have disabilities. Either the student himself or his parents are being judged by God for some sin.

The Lord Jesus refuted this line of thinking in His day, however. In John 9, we read the account of a blind man. The disciples, like many people today, had surmised that the man's blindness was a reflection of God's hand of judgment for someone's sin, for they asked, "Master, who did sin, this man, or his parents, that he was born blind?" Christ, correcting them immediately, said, "Neither hath this man sinned, nor his parents: but that the works of God should be made manifest in him." We believe that God is simply glorified in His creation of children with disabilities.

We cannot infer from this passage, however, that absolutely no disabilities can ever be the result of sin. God may in fact choose to disable a student in some way for continual, unconfessed sin. However, we must be careful not to appoint ourselves judge and jury and withhold appropriate education from a disabled child just because we may believe his disability is a result of sin. After all, God does not withhold spiritual remediation (i.e., salvation) from unrighteous, *spiritually impaired* man. Therefore, we should emulate our God. We need to ensure that disabled children receive instruction that meets their unique needs, be it educational or spiritual. If the individualized (special) education that we are providing struggling learners is Bible-based and emphasizes spiritual truth, then all of their needs, spiritual and otherwise, will be sufficiently met.

We must reconsider how we view children with disabilities. To look at them (or their parents) in a skeptical way as if they might have possibly committed some great sin and that they may be suffering God's judgment will surely taint our dealings and interactions with them. We give these children far too little credit in being able to read the true feelings and emotions we hold toward them and their disabilities. They are indeed more perceptive than what we may think. Accepting students with disabilities as the unique creation of God that they are is the best position to take. The Psalmist wrote, "for we are fearfully and wonderfully made" (Ps. 139:14) and "His way is perfect" (Ps. 18:30). We agree with Behymer, who has stated that "When God chooses to allow a disability to [exist and] remain, He is best glorified by our acceptance of the person as God made him."[4]

Principle 3

Students with disabilities must learn Truth and gain spiritual understanding. It is the primary obligation of parents who have children with disabilities to teach Truth (II Tim. 2:2; Prov. 8:6-9). The fact that the child has a disability and may be viewed by the world as different does not change the fact that home educators are bound and obligated to teach Truth. It matters not the type or the severity of the child's disability. The home teacher's obligation is to teach Truth, and the disabled student must learn Truth.

What is Truth? The Scriptures indicate that the Word of God is Truth (Jn. 17:17), the Holy Spirit is Truth (Jn. 16:13), the fear of the Lord is Truth (Prov. 1:7), and the Lord Jesus Himself is Truth (Jn 14:6). There are many educational approaches that will remediate a child's learning and behavior problems (we will discuss these in later chapters), but there is only one way to correct a child's sin problem and that is through the Lord Jesus Christ, who is the Way, the Truth, and the Life. Our first and foremost spiritual obligation in teaching children with disabilities in home schools is to see them accept the Lord Jesus as their personal Savior and be saved.

The teaching of Truth must permeate everything that a parent would teach a disabled child in the home, and Truth must be reinforced continually, making home education for struggling learners distinctively and thoroughly Christian. The methods the teacher employs should be ones that are capable of conveying Truth. But methods are a means to an end, that end being the teaching and acceptance of Truth. Not all methods used by special educators are a means of teaching Truth. For example, secular humanistic approaches like reality therapy and life space interviewing,[5] which are counseling interventions that do not hold the student ultimately accountable for his behavior, have no place in a Christian home program.

Bringing children to a saving knowledge of Christ is not the culminating end of all spiritual teaching in the home school. Parents must continue teaching Truth so that children with disabilities will gain spiritual understanding (Prov. 14:6; Prov. 18:1; Prov. 2:3-5). As part of their spiritual growth, parents should help disabled children understand their uniqueness as God's own creation and that He made them with a purpose in mind. Children with disabilities desperately need to understand that they are not freaks or accidents of nature. They will need to learn fully of the great God who loves them supremely and unconditionally.

Principle 4

Students with disabilities must learn Christlikeness and acquire godly character. Some parents believe that children with disabilities should be placed on a different educational agenda. That is, we should be teaching radically different things to disabled children since they often show so many differences from their nondisabled counterparts. This is simply not the case. Skill for skill, ability for ability, we believe there are more likenesses and similarities between children with disabilities and those that are nondisabled than there are differences. Therefore, we hold that what children with disabilities are to learn should not be that different from what nondisabled children learn.

Like nondisabled children, children with disabilities need to learn Christian character and how to live godly lives for the Lord. This is, in fact, the primary purpose of our teaching in the home. This differs markedly from what secular educators believe the main goal of education to be. Instead, they believe that getting children ready to make a contribution to this world, teaching them how to earn money in order to pay bills, or helping them become literate are the most important reasons of education. Although none of these goals are inherently evil, these are secondary to the primary purpose of building Christian character in our children's lives.

We know that Christian character in disabled children will be manifested though their inward relationship with God and their outward relationship with man. For example, in relation to God, it is important that disabled children, like their nondisabled counterparts, learn to glorify God in all that they do and accomplish (I Cor. 10:31), love the Lord with all their hearts (Deut. 6:5; Matt. 22:37), obey the Lord right away and at all times (II Cor. 10:5), recognize that they can only be made complete in Him (II Tim. 3:17), and refrain from self-service and self-centeredness (Phil. 2:3-5). In relation to man, we should teach children with disabilities to obey their parents (Eph. 6:1), to love one another (Matt. 22:39), to refrain from offending others (I Cor. 10:32; II Cor. 6:3), and to do good unto all men (Gal. 6:10).

Principle 5

Students with disabilities must recognize their God-given abilities and place of service to the Lord. We must bring children with disabilities to the point in their spiritual lives that they recognize that they are indeed not their own and that they are bought with a price, that price being the life blood of the Lord Jesus Himself (Rom 12:1-2; I Cor. 6:20). The purchase of our lives by the Lord Jesus' death means that we are to serve Him for the remainder of our days on this earth in whatever field of service that He calls us, and it should be done lovingly and not begrudgingly.

Children, disabled and nondisabled alike, will need to learn that God has a purpose for each and every person's life. Parents must teach continually two very important truths. One, articulated by Vaughn, is that "Every child has everything he needs in order to do God's will for his life."[6] We must not incorrectly surmise that, because a child has a *disability*, he has no *abilities* with which to serve God. To the contrary, we know that "every man hath received the gift" (I Peter 4:10), and this does *not* exclude those with disabilities. Each one has a gift with which to serve God and minister to others. The Lord will not call all to preach or teach. He won't call all to be engineers or lawyers. Whatever the calling or gift, though, God will equip and empower each person to serve as He wills.

A second related truth, originated by Dr. Bob Jones, Sr., is that "For a Christian, life is not divided into the secular and the sacred. To him all ground is holy ground..."[7] No one calling, then, is more important in God's sight than another calling. Students with disabilities must recognize that their calling of God will be sacred, too. The service they render to the Lord will be just as unique, just as needed, and will produce a savor that is just as sweet as that rendered by nondisabled individuals whom the Lord calls. The place of service in which the Lord places a disabled individual may not be as prominent as that of other nondisabled people, but it is still an important place of service nonetheless. Behymer aptly writes:

> Unfortunately, earthly ideas of success still dominate our thinking. We often establish a person's value by how much he earns, owns, or contributes to society. For example, the status of a physician is generally thought of as higher than that of a street sweeper. These attitudes could not be

farther from the truth shown in God's Word....It is not up to us to decide whether or not a disabled person's contribution in life is worth something....We are to look at disabled people as God does and do our best to help each one reach the full potential that God has given him.[8]

Emulating the Master Teacher

The Scriptures are replete with examples of different methods God used to teach His people. His methods many times included objects of His own creation. For example, He used a *tree* to teach Adam and Eve in the Garden of Eden about the eternal consequences of disobedience (Gen. 3:17). He used a rainbow to teach the small remnant of people who survived with Noah that He would never again use a universal flood to destroy the earth (Gen. 9:13-15). He used the *tabernacle* in the Old Testament to teach of the Savior, the Lord Jesus, to come (Heb. 9:11). When the scribes and pharisees brought the adulteress before the Lord Jesus in an effort to tempt and accuse Him, Christ's method of pronouncing judgment on these men included stooping down and *writing on the ground* (Jn. 8:6).

But the ultimate teaching method in all of Scripture is the plan of salvation God used to redeem sinful man. In short, God the Father used His only begotten Son, Christ Jesus, to accomplish this plan. For those who know the Lord Jesus as Savior, the specific elements of salvation are simple and precious. God loved us so much that He sent His Son from the regal glories of heaven to earth so that He would die and intercede for pitiful, sinful men (Jn. 3:16). The Lord Jesus humbled Himself, took on the form of a servant and the likeness of a man, and gave up His life on a cruel, rugged cross to pay sin's price for all men and women, past, present, and future (Phil. 2:6-8). God's method of salvation does not end here, for the Scripture tell us that God raised Him (Christ) from the dead (Acts 2:32), and He lives today and forevermore as the Mediator between God and men (I Tim. 2:5).

Christ Himself stands as the Master Teacher of individuals with limitations. His method was unique and His example worth emulating. From two specific accounts of Christ's ministry, both having to do with disabled persons—one with *blindness* (John 9:1-7), the other with *palsy* (Mark 2:1-5, 10-12)—we discover keys to how parents should meet the needs of struggling learners. Although Christ had other encounters with disabled individuals (see Figure 2.1), we believe these two accounts provide the best picture of how He taught them. Consider first the account of the blind man in John 9:1-7. The passage reads:

> And as Jesus passed by, he saw a man which was blind from his birth. And his disciples asked him, saying, Master, who did sin, this man or his parents, that he was born blind? Jesus answered, Neither hath this man sinned, nor his parents: but that the works of God should be made manifest in him. I must work the works of him that sent me, while it is day: the night cometh, when no man can work. As long as I am in the world, I am the light of the world. When he had thus spoken he spat on the ground, and made clay of the spittle, and he anointed the eyes of the blind man with the clay. And said unto him, Go, wash in the pool of Siloam, (which is by interpretation, Sent.) He went his way, therefore, and washed, and came seeing.

The second passage relaying the palsied man's experience with Christ is found in Mark 2:1-5, 10-12. It reads as follows:

> And again he [Christ] entered into Capernaum, after some days, and it was noised that he was in the house. And straightway many were gathered together, insomuch that there was no room to receive them, no, not so much as about the door: and he preached the word unto them. And they came unto him, bringing one sick of the palsy, which was borne of four, And when they could not come nigh unto him for the press, they uncovered the roof where he was: and when they had broken it up, they let down the bed wherein the sick of the palsy lay. When Jesus saw their faith, He said unto the sick of the palsy, Son, thy sins be forgiven thee. [verses 10-12] But that ye may know that the Son of man hath power on earth to forgive sins, (he saith to the sick of the palsy), I say unto thee, Arise, and take up thy bed, and go thy way into thine house. And immediately he arose, took up the bed, and went forth before them all...

Figure 2.1

Accounts of Christ with Disabled Persons

Disability	References
Blind (VI)	Matt. 9:27-31; Matt. 20:29-34; Mk. 8:22-26; Mk. 10:46-52; Lk. 18:35-43; Jn. 9:1-7, 35-38
Blind/Lame (VI/PI)	Matt. 14:21
Deaf/Dumb (HI/CD)	Mk. 7:32-37
Dropsy (PI)	Lk. 14:1-6
Epilepsy (PI)	Matt. 17:14-21; Mk. 9:17-27; Lk. 9:37-42
Infirmity (PI)	Lk. 13:10-17; Jn. 4:1-16
Issue of Blood (OHI)	Matt. 9:18-22; Mk. 5:25-34; Lk. 8:43-48
Lame/Blind/Dumb/ Maimed (MD)	Matt. 16:30-31
Leprosy (PI)	Matt. 8:1-4; Mk. 1:40-45; Lk. 5:12-16; Lk. 17:11-19
Lunatic (EBD)	Matt. 4:24
Palsy (PI)	Matt. 8:5-13; Matt. 9:1-8; Mk. 2:1-12; Lk. 5:18-26; Lk. 7:1-10
Withered Hand (PI)	Matt. 12:9-13; Mk. 3:1-5; Lk. 6:6-11

Legend: CD=Communication Disorder; EBD=Emotional-Behavior Disorder HI=Hearing Impairment; OHI=Other Health Impairment; MD=Multiple Disabilities; PI=Physical Impairment; VI=Visual Impairment.

Careful examination of both of these passages allow us to make several observations on how the Lord provided for the needs of those with disabilities. We can extract three elements from His teaching that should be part of one's framework for teaching struggling learners: (1) one-on-one instruction; (2) methods tailored to needs; and (3) alternative assessment.[9]

One-on-One Instruction

Individual, one-on-one instruction was foremost in Christ's dealings with these two disabled men. His verbal interaction with them was in a pure one-on-one fashion, as opposed to his typical style of preaching to the masses. For each of these men, Christ performed two miracles in their lives— He saved them from their sins, and He made them physically whole again. God still deals with us today as individuals, does He not? He still saves us as individuals, He forgives us individually of our sins, and He meets all of our individual needs.

Children with disabilities more often than not will need one-on-one attention and instruction if they are to succeed educationally. It matters not what disability they have. If it has an adverse effect on the child's ability to learn and achieve, then the child in all likelihood will need some degree of individualized instruction.

Interestingly, individualized education is at the very heart of what special education programming was intended to be in our public schools.[10,11] Moreover, individualized education for all students with disabilities in the form of *individualized educational plans* (IEP) is the intent of the *free appropriate public education* provision that was mandated in the 1975 federal special education law, Public Law 94-142.[12] This mandate, of course, was reiterated again in the 1990 reauthorization bill, Public Law 101-476, better known as the Individuals with Disabilities Education Act.[13]

Unfortunately, a mandated individualized education does not necessarily translate into individualized instruction per se. In fact, in most public schools, individualized education for children with disabilities is delivered in small group settings (called *resource* or *self-contained* classrooms). Teacher-student ratios in these special education classes will vary based on state mandated guidelines. But we know one thing for sure. The teacher-student ratio in most public school special education classrooms will not be 1:1 (i.e., one teacher to one student). Even recommendations from scholars in the field go well beyond a 1:1 teacher-student ratio. For example, Zacherman[14] recommends a 1:5 ratio, while Reger[15] says it should be 1:3 or 1:4, and Zimmerman[16] believes that some children with disabilities can survive quite nicely in larger groups where the student-teacher ratio is between 1:7 and 1:10.

Clearly, parents have the advantage over conventional special educators in providing one-on-one instruction. We agree with Somerville[17] that there is no better or more convenient educational setting than the home to provide individualized, one-on-one instruction. White, citing the benefits of the home instructional setting for ADD students, states that, "the child does not have to contend with the noise and distractions of...other students."[18] In a first study of its kind to determine the effectiveness of home instruction with learning disabled students, Duvall concluded that parents, "provided powerful instructional environments at home that...[made] significant improvements in [LD students'] basic skills."[19] He cited low student numbers in home schools as an integral part of these students' success.

Methods Tailored to Needs

When we analyze the two Scripture passages further, we find that Christ did more for these two disabled men than just provide one-on-one instruction. He used special teaching methods, unconventional in His day and time, that were tailored to meet the needs of each man. Parents of struggling learners will need to do the same if they ever hope to see these children improve.

Most Christians will readily conclude that Christ, the Master Teacher, understood and practiced special education long before secular educators of the twentieth century. The current concept of *remediation* (discussed in more detail in Chapter 4), which is central to special education programming, has to do with correcting a child's learning gaps and skill deficits by using special teaching methods. Christ implemented special methods with both disabled men in order to meet their physical and spiritual needs.

For the blind man, Christ "made clay of the spittle, and He anointed the eyes of the blind man with the clay." For the palsied man, his bed-bearers "uncovered the roof where [Christ] was...and they let down the bed" of the palsied man so Christ could deal with him. In both cases, Christ's method in dealing with the men, both spiritually and physically, was uniquely tailored to work around their limitations and meet their unique needs. In short, Christ altered how he usually taught (i.e., to the masses) in order to help these disabled men.

One of the problems that conventional special educators face daily is finding the necessary time to develop and implement individualized programs, methods, and instructional modifications for each of their students. The task is almost insurmountable when the teacher's case load of students is factored in. For example, in Virginia public schools, some resource special education teachers serve as many as 24 different children with disabilities over the course of a school day.[20]

Once again, the teaching parent has the advantage over conventional special educators in tailoring methods to children's needs. The typical family will probably have no more than one or two children with bona fide disabilities (although it is possible for some families to have several struggling learners); hence, there is ample time for parents to identify the characteristics and needs of the child and choose or plan methods that are appropriate for him/her.

Alternative Assessment

The third and final provision made for the blind man and the palsied man by the Lord Jesus was alternative assessment. How Christ evaluated the changes in these two men was unique, and His assessment in each case corresponded to the characteristic difficulties and limitations that accompanied each man's disability. In both cases, the *mode* of and the *response* to assessment was altered from the usual to assess improvement.

For the blind man, Christ instructed him to "Go...[and]...wash in the pool of Siloam." It was upon obedience to this action that the blind man "went his way, therefore, washed, and came seeing." The evaluation mode was a pool of water; the evaluation response was washing. For the palsied man, Christ instructed him to "Arise, and take up [his] bed, and go [his] way into [his] house," upon which the man "immediately...arose, took up the bed, and went forth before them all." The evaluation mode in this case was the bed; the evaluation response was taking up the bed and walking.

Parents who choose to teach their disabled children at home may also need to develop alternative assessment techniques. For example, a child with a learning disability in writing may need to be evaluated differently in almost every subject. While paper-and-pencil type of assessment, from seat work assignments, to worksheets, to quizzes, to unit tests are the traditional way of informally assessing student progress, there is nothing written (pun unintended!) in stone that says it has to be written. This child could simply speak his answers to questions, and the parent would be able to assess his mastery.

Once more, we believe the teaching parent has the edge over conventional special educators in providing alternative assessment. In all likelihood, home teachers may have more flexible schedules and smaller case loads, which will enable them to provide and ad minister alternative evaluation procedures more readily and more effectively.

One-on-One is not Enough

We have had some to suggest that one-on-one instruction is perhaps all that is needed to meet the unique needs of students with disabilities. Our position is that one-on-one instruction is not enough. The highly individualized nature of home schools suggests that some one-on-one instruction is already going on. So, if effectiveness indeed hinges solely on one-on-one instruction, then why are struggling learners still struggling? And if all children (i.e., those that struggle and those that don't) are recipients of the routine one-on-one instruction that is available in the home, then what exactly is being done above and beyond the usual for the struggling learner?

Our view is that parents who limit their programming for struggling learners to one-on-one instruction are much like soldiers who use only guns in warfare, but ignore other battle gear such as helmets, knives, hand grenades, tear gas, etc. While these soldiers may win a few skirmishes, chances are, that without full battle regalia, they may likely lose the war. Guns are powerful, effective weapons, but a soldier's ability to fight effectively is clearly magnified when he equips himself as completely as possible with other weapons and defensive equipment.

Similarly, we don't deny that one-on-one instruction is a powerful tool. We concur with the Home School Legal Defense Association that the home school environment provides for an "enhanced opportunity to individualize curriculum and methodology..."[21] But teaching struggling learners is no easy task, and no single intervention, not even one-on-one instruction, is enough to overcome the significant learning, attention, and behavior difficulties these children have. However, supplementing one-on-one instruction with carefully tailored teaching methods and alternative assessment, just as Christ did, will intensify overall instructional efforts and allow greater opportunities for struggling learners to succeed.

[1]American Heritage Dictionary (1985)
[2]Vaughn (1993a), p. 21
[3]Spain (1986)
[4]Behymer (1993), p. 289
[5]Heuchert & Long (1980)
[6]Vaughn (1993b)
[7]Jones (no date), p. 5
[8]Behymer (1993), p. 290
[9]J. Sutton (1993a)
[10]Hallahan & Kauffman (1991)
[11]C. Mercer & A. Mercer (1993)
[12]U.S. Department of Education (1975)
[13]U.S. Department of Education (1990)
[14]Zacherman (1992)
[15]Reger (1973)
[16]Zimmerman (1982)
[17]Somerville (1994)
[18]White (1994), p. 46
[19]Duvall (1994), p. 11
[20]J. Sutton (1989)
[21]Home School Legal Defense Association (1990), p. 5

Chapter

3

Testing and Evaluation

Not all experiences in life are easy and enjoyable. There will be hard and stressful times that we all have to endure as we grow and mature. Testing is one example. Many parents bristle at the very mention of it, for they, like countless others, have been subjected to the demands and rigors of testing at one time or another during their school years. Testing nonetheless has played a critical role in the education of children throughout history.

Unfortunately, testing is typically viewed as a final measure of a child's learning *after* instruction has taken place. But in teaching struggling learners, testing and evaluation can play a much more powerful role. It can be used as a *beginning* step in planning effective instruction. But beyond learning about how it can be used instructionally, we believe there may be a more compelling reason why parents, particularly those who have struggling learners, should learn about testing and evaluation.

During our speaking engagements at state and national home school conventions over the last several years, we have become acquainted with scores of parents who expressed dissatisfaction with testing services they had received from professional diagnosticians. Many admitted that, because they had no understanding of even the basic essentials of testing and evaluation, they had unintentionally contracted for testing that, in the long-run, produced little more than a technical written report with meaningless scores and professional jargon. Simply put, individual educational testing for struggling learners is not only complex, but it can be expensive. We believe parents would be in a better position to make wiser, more sound decisions if they are knowledgeable about the basics of testing and evaluation.

The remainder of this chapter, then, will be devoted to the following topics related to testing struggling learners: (a) reasons for testing; (b) specific types of tests; (c) qualifications of diagnosticians; (d) timeline for testing; and (e) the cost factor.

Reasons for Testing

Our position is that struggling learners need individual educational testing and evaluation. But we are not recommending testing just to make life more difficult or financially burdensome for parents or just to be in keeping with what conventional educators are doing. To the contrary, if parents understand testing properly and if findings are implemented correctly, then instruction should be easier to plan and evaluate in the long run. Struggling learners need individual testing and evaluation for four primary reasons: (1) identifying a disability; (2) determining functioning level; (3) diagnosing skill deficits; and (4) documenting progress.

Identifying a Disability

Virtually all children will show some difficulties in learning, attention, and behavior throughout their grade school years. For example, it would not be unusual for a parent to observe a younger child (or even an older student!) daydreaming several times during the course of one school week. But with a small segment of the school-age population, difficulties in learning, attention, and behavior can be more frequent and persistent. Not only do these difficulties remain across time, but they may even worsen as the child matures. Consider the following letter we received some time ago from one home educating mother:

> I really feel at the end of my rope with my son sometimes. He's a wonderful, loving, caring boy, but at times I just don't know what I am doing wrong. It has only lately

occurred to me that he may have a learning disability. He has always out-performed his sister scholastically (and she's two years his senior). Some of the things that he has already learned I have never taught him. He has just been able to pick it up on his own (e.g., reading, relationships of math facts to one another, etc.).

But when I think of the lengths I have had to go to extract that information from him...the constant prodding (and I mean constant!) to complete the next assigned task, urging him to think about what he's doing...it simply dazzles me. I can't explain any other way how a child can remember exact details from events that occurred when he turned two, yet he cannot remember which direction the silverware drawer is when he is setting the table.

No discipline or reward system, or any other method I (or my husband) have tried seems to help. Just recently, we spent hours doing one load of laundry. Actually he spent hours trying to do it, and I spent hours reminding, correcting, setting timers, disciplining, and generally just being frustrated with him. I've always taken this as something that is "normal," a typical behavior for a boy (his sisters never did things like this!). I've even thought that it could be a discipline problem with him but one that he would grow out of one day. But IT'S NOT GOING AWAY.,,,So often I have wondered if I have failed him in some way because of the way I am (or am not) teaching him.

No doubt this mother was observing learning and behavior problems that were beyond what typical children experience. But how can a parent know if a child's problems are *more frequent* and *extreme* from those of other typical children? One way would be to conduct an informal home test.

Suppose, for example, that a parent decides to observe and record her son's inattention over the course of four to six weeks and concludes that he is off-task and inattentive about 50% of the time. The parent further notes that the child did not appear to be intentionally not paying attention. Based on this small amount of informal, observational data, the parent *may* rightfully infer that this degree of inattention is beyond what we might expect of a typical child and that such behavior *could* be indicative of an attention deficit disorder (See Chapter 1). But only through formal testing and evaluation can parents know for sure whether a child's learning, attention, and behavior problems are rooted in some form of disability.

Identifying a child's disability for instructional purposes can be likened unto diagnosing a physical illness. Suppose that your child has been suffering from stomach pains for several days. He has great difficulty keeping his food down. He looks increasingly pale and weak. He is sluggish in his work and play, and he tells you that he would rather lie in bed and rest than go out and play. You observe that these symptoms persist for several days in succession.

Few loving, caring parents would leave such a child to himself, hoping and praying that he will simply shake off these serious, potentially life-threatening symptoms. Let's face it. Most parents would yield to the expertise and counsel of a medical doctor to examine the child thoroughly and anxiously await a diagnosis of the problem. Moreover, most would proceed quickly to secure whatever medical assistance is necessary to bring the child back to full health.

Should parents do any less when their child shows signs of diminished performance in learning, attention, and behavior? Should they ignore children who are suffering in their school performance, not able to excel in their school work, failing to master the skills they are being taught? Should parents overlook it when children grow pale and weak in their enthusiasm and motivation for learning and when they are sluggish at improving in their studies and actions for prolonged periods of time? When children are able to do well in many other activities of their lives, but just can't seem to perform academically and behaviorally up to par, should parents pretend that such symptoms will not have an adverse effect on the child's academic success and self-concept in the long run?

Our view is that parents should not ignore persistent educational and behavioral problems in their children. Just as diagnosis and cure of medical problems are vital to the continuing good health and physical development of a child, so it is critically important that a child's disability be identified as early as possible.[1] The sooner we can pinpoint and define the specific disability that may be preventing a child from succeeding, the sooner we will understand how God made him and can move on to developing an educational program that will meet his unique needs.

Testing for the purpose of identifying a child's disability is typically called a *psychological* or *psychoeducational evaluation*. Vergason defines an *evaluation* as "an appraisal or estimation of certain specific characteristics, such as intelligence, personality, or physical aspects of an individual."[2] In essence, a diagnostician will administer a battery of different one-on-one tests that measure the child's intelligence, achievement, perceptual-motor skills, adaptive behavior skills, speech-language skills, behavior, attention skills, and so on (We discuss these different types of tests in the sections that follow.) The diagnostician will also collect other informal data on the child (e.g., parent observations of the child's school performance, samples of school work, medical records, other background information, etc.)

Once all formal and informal data on the child have been collected, the diagnostician will conduct an in-depth analysis and provide a written report of findings and recommendations to the parent. A proper evaluation report should provide the following information about the child: (1) background information; (2) observations of behavior during testing; (3) a list of specific tests administered; (4) actual test scores (e.g., grade equivalents, percentile ranks, etc.); (5) interpretation of test scores; (6) a firm, clear, substantiated decision regarding the presence or absence of a disability; (7) extent of special education programming needed ; and (8) some instructional recommendations.

The primary purpose of this type of testing, then, is to identify and verify the presence of a disability in the child, *not* to provide extensive diagnostic and instructional recommendations on how a home education program should be tailored for the child. Therefore, parents should come away from the evaluation with a complete understanding of whether or not their child has a disability and the specific nature of it. With these test results, parents will know better how to set *reasonable expectations* for their child. Probably one of the most important benefits from psychoeducational testing is that parents will no longer feel personally responsible for the child's lack of success. If test results indicate a disability, then parents must accept the fact that God may be pleased for the child to have a limitation (See Chapter 2 and our discussion of Principle 2.)

Determining Functioning Level

As we have stated earlier, parents need to develop tailor-made programs of instruction for struggling learners. We recommend that the program include two major strands of teaching: (1) *remedial* instruction for closing the learning gaps; and (2) *regular* instruction for teaching the traditional scope and sequence of skills expected of students at that child's age. Children with disabilities will not be able to achieve at optimal levels and progress educationally if they receive only regular instruction. The remedial strand of teaching will be critical, but it is no more important than the regular curriculum teaching strand, and vice versa. Both forms of instruction are essential for children with disabilities. (Refer to Chapter 4 for a more comprehensive discussion of these two strands of instruction.)

To maximize their success in regular instruction, children with disabilities should study from curricular materials (i.e., textbooks, workbooks, etc.) that are at a *functioning* or *instructional* level, not *frustrational* level of learning.[3] Many times we find these children studying from materials that are considerably higher than their current level of skill functioning. The end result is a frustrated child, whose overall school performance is less than satisfactory, sometimes failure. We illustrate the difference in levels of learning with the following example.

David has a learning disability, and his chronological grade placement (or grade assignment) is fifth grade (i.e., he has completed kindergarten and four grade school years). Because of David's accompanying learning problems, he is not achieving at fifth grade level in most of his subjects. To the contrary, David, like many other children with mild forms of disability, is functioning at grade levels that are below his current grade assignment. Having him learn from grade level curricula that are at his fifth grade placement will most likely be a frustrational learning experience for him. On the other hand, placing him on grade level materials per subject area that are at his current functioning level will allow him to move forward at a more successful, less frustrational pace. Herein we see the second reason why testing and evaluation is important for students with disabilities— to determine their present level of functioning or achievement. Specifically, the scores from the one-on-one achievement tests administered by a diagnostician will serve as a guideline for placing the student on an appropriate standard curricula. We continue with our scenario of David to illustrate.

Suppose David earned a grade equivalent (G.E.) score of 2.8 in reading decoding (pronunciation) and a G.E. of 3.2 in reading comprehension on a one-on-one administered achievement test. Grade equivalent scores, like age equivalent scores, compare the individual child's performance to that of a large, representative sample of students across the country who were involved in the field-testing of the achievement test.

We interpret David's score in reading decoding to mean that his performance is comparable to that of average students in the norm sample who were in the eighth month of their second grade year in school (i.e., G.E. of 2.8). In like manner, we interpret David's score in reading comprehension to mean that his performance was comparable to that of average students in the norm sample who were in the second month of their third grade year (i.e., G.E. of 3.2). Based on these scores, then, the third grade level would serve as a better estimate of David's functioning or instructional level in reading than his fifth grade assignment. His parents should, therefore, choose a regular curriculum in reading that reflects a third grade level.

Although principles of psychometry[4] do not allow us to infer directly that a grade equivalent score, in fact, represents a child's absolute functioning level, we can use it as a guideline. Some parents may determine that using curricular materials that are one grade level above (or below) the child's grade equivalent score would be a closer estimate of his true functioning level. It is important that parents make informed judgments about choice of educational materials in their home programs. Using the grade equivalent as a guideline is a way to avoid arbitrary decisions.

Diagnosing Skill Deficits

A second form of testing, sometimes referred to as a *diagnostic skill evaluation*, generally follows a psychoeducational evaluation. A diagnostic evaluation will include a number of one-on-one administered, in-depth diagnostic tests designed to pinpoint a child's academic skill deficits. Findings from a diagnostic evaluation will subsequently be used in planning remedial instruction.

Here is how diagnostic testing works. If a student has been found to have a learning disability in reading decoding skills, a diagnostic evaluation would be administered to identify his specific reading decoding skill deficits, which may include deficiencies in short or long vowel sounds, digraphs, beginning consonant sounds, phonetic irregularities, and so on. Similarly, if a student is found to have significant weaknesses in mathematics, a diagnostic evaluation would pinpoint his skill deficits across the different math domains including computation, application, time, measurement, geometric concepts, fractions, and so on.

Diagnostic testing differs markedly from psychoeducational testing. The latter will generally assess the child's level of skill attainment only, which is typically communicated to the parent in the form of quantitative or normative scores. Examples would include grade equivalent scores (e.g., 3.4—third grade, fourth month), age equivalent scores (e.g., 9-5—nine years, 5 months), standard scores (e.g., 107—where the mean score is 100), and percentile ranks (e.g., 58th—which means the child performed better than 57% of the norm sample). The primary purpose of psychoeducational testing, then, is to compare a child's ability and performance with a comparison group of his age peers. Very little instructional information about the child's mastery of *specific* academic skills can be gleaned from psychoeducational testing, although parents do get a good handle of the child's overall skill attainment.

Diagnostic tests, on the other hand, assess a child's skill mastery of a standard body of skills expected of typical children who are at the same assigned grade level as the child. The only resulting quantitative score may be a simple count or percentage of how many skills the child *actually* knows versus the number of skills he *should* know. In short, a diagnostic skill evaluation will generate a list of academic skills that the child has mastered and, more important, those in which he has not yet shown proficiency or mastery. The list of skills in which the child has not shown mastery can provide the home teacher with specific direction in *what* to teach the child during remedial instruction. Some diagnosticians will also include some teaching recommendations, which, of course, address the second requirement in remedial instruction, namely, *how* to teach the child. (See the methods chapters in this book for teaching ideas.)

By way of illustration, we have listed in Figure 3.1 the specific capitalization skills in which third grade and ninth grade students would be expected to show mastery (as taken from the *Brigance Diagnostic Comprehensive Inventory of Basic Skills*[5]). The number of skills will vary based on the child's assigned grade level. Students in lower elementary grades would not be expected to show mastery of as many academic skills as those in middle or high school.

Figure 3.1

Capitalization Skills for Two Grade Levels

Third Grade	Ninth Grade*
• First word in sentence	• Bodies of water and landforms
• Pronoun "I"	• Special groups of people
• Names of people	• First word in direct quotation
• Days of the week	• Continents
• Special days/holidays	• Titles of books/stories/magazines
• Months of the year	• Business firms, brand names
• Streets and roadways	• Government groups
• Cities	• Proper adjectives
• States	• Historical events and periods
• Countries	• Religions and nationalities
• Titles of people	• Directions as regions
• Initials	• Ships, trains, and planes

*Ninth grade students learn these capitalization skills in addition to those expected of third graders.

Documenting Progress

Parents, like teachers in conventional schools, will want to know whether their children are achieving and progressing as they should. One way of documenting progress is through daily informal measures, which would include percentage-correct scores from worksheets, tests, projects, and the like. We will address how students with disabilities should be evaluated on an informal, daily basis in Chapter 5.

For students with disabilities, formal documentation of progress is accomplished through *one-on-one* administered achievement tests or diagnostic tests (note the following section for recommended tests).

Generally, individually administered achievement tests will only need to be administered once a year, preferably near the end of the school year, between the months of April and June. Parents would compare the child's current achievement test scores with scores earned on the same or similar test administered the prior year.

The figures provided in Figure 3.2 are the annual achievement scores from two consecutive years of a learning disabled student (seventh grade; age 12 years, 6 months), using selected subtests from the *Woodcock-Johnson Psycho-Educational Battery-Tests of Achievement.*[6] Sometimes one-on-one standardized achievement test scores do not adequately show academic progress, nor do they always do justice in describing the successful learning of a child with a disability. For this reason, diagnostic test results may be more preferable. As mentioned earlier, diagnostic tests do not generally produce the full array of standardized scores as norm-referenced achievement tests do. But diagnostic tests have the advantage of showing in a more vivid way the progress that a child has made by providing a count of specific skills mastered.

Figure 3.2

Achievement Scores of an LD Student

	Age Equivalent		Grade Equivalent		Percentile Rank	
Academic Skill	1992	1993	1992	1993	1992	1993
Letter-Word Identification	8-10	11-7	3.6	6.2	16	39
Passage Comprehension	10-10	13-8	5.6	8.3	42	65
Mathematics Calculation	10-4	11-3	5.0	5.9	22	27

We illustrate by reexamining the learning disabled student's achievement scores in mathematics calculation provided in Figure 3.2. A comparison of the child's age equivalent, grade equivalent, and particularly her percentile rank scores do not reveal very much progress beyond normal development after one year. But consider in Figure 3.3 the change in the number of math skills mastered by this same learning disabled student from her diagnostic evaluation (note that the fractions in each column represent the number of questions answered correctly out of the total possible from the *KeyMath Revised: A Diagnostic Inventory of Essential Mathematics*[7]).

Figure 3.3

Diagnostic Math Scores of an LD Student

Math Skill	1992	1993	Percent
Numeration	14/21	17/21	+14.3%
Fractions	5/8	5/8	0%
Geometry/Symbols	17/18	17/18	0%
Addition	13/14	11/14	- 14.3%
Subtraction	8/11	10/11	+18.2%
Multiplication	5/10	9/10	+40.0%
Division	4/8	6/8	+25.0%
Mental Computation	4/10	6/10	+20.0%
Numerical Reasoning	7/10	10/10	+30.0%
Word Problems	7/11	7/11	0%
Money	9/11	9/11	0%
Measurement	15/23	17/23	+ 8.7%
Time	9/19	10/10	+ 5.3%

When combined, both standardized achievement scores and diagnostic test results provide a more complete and detailed picture of progress. Given that academic progress may come more slowly for students with disabilities, parents may find it more beneficial and encouraging, then, to have both types of testing done on a regular basis.

Specific Types of Tests

Tests can be either formal or informal. Formal tests for students with disabilities fall into three main categories: (1) psychoeducational tests; (2) diagnostic skill tests; and (3) achievement tests. These types of tests must be administered individually by a professional diagnostician. Two other types of tests screening—tests and learning style evaluations—are considered more formal than informal forms of assessment, but they can be administered in the home by the parent, under the supervision of a diagnostician. Finally, parents can develop and administer informal tests to their children.

There is significance in using individual, one-on-one administered tests with struggling learners. Luftig states that group-administered tests (e.g., *Stanford Achievement Test-8th Edition*[8]) typically administered in whole-group settings require that students "possess strong reading or listening skills as well as skill in following directions and working independently,"[9] skills we know that children with disabilities generally do not sufficiently possess. Individually-administered one-on-one tests also allow the examiner more flexibility and control in making sure that the disabled student does understand directions by giving additional cues and prompts to the student as necessary, which should result in a more accurate measure of the child's abilities and achievement. With group-administered achievement tests, however, the diagnostician is *not* allowed to deviate from the scripted instructions in the administration manual.

One other major advantage of one-on-one tests is that test items which allow the student to guess (quite prevalent in group-administered achievement tests) are all but eliminated. For example, spelling test items on group-administered achievement tests typically present the child with four renditions of a spelling word. He then is instructed to pick the one which is spelled correctly. Probability tells us that the child has a 25% chance of guessing the item correctly. One-on-one administered spelling tests, however, require the child to write out each spelling word from recall.

Psychoeducational Tests

Psychoeducational evaluations typically include, but are not limited to, individual tests of intelligence, achievement, adaptive behavior, and perceptual-motor skills, as well as speech-language skills surveys and emotional-behavior, attention, and giftedness rating scales. All of these tests can be administered to the child at one sitting or across several sessions and days. Each of these types of tests is described below with specific examples.

Intelligence Tests. Intelligence tests assess a student's God-given abilities to think, reason, remember, process information, acquire knowledge, and the like. The resulting IQ (intelligence quotient) score is a reflection of the student's *potential* to learn. The most popularly used one-on-one intelligence tests follow.

- *Wechsler Intelligence Scale for Children-Third Edition*[10]

- *Stanford-Binet Intelligence Scale*[11]
- *Woodcock-Johnson Psycho-Educational Battery-Tests of Cognitive Abilities*[12]
- *Kaufman Assessment Battery for Children*[13]
- *Detroit Test of Learning Aptitude-Third Revision*[14]

Achievement Tests. Achievement tests determine the child's current level of performance in the reading/language arts and mathematics areas. Scores reflect what the child has actually learned in the academic skill areas, not what he is able to learn. The most commonly used one-on-one achievement tests are listed below:

- *Wechsler Individual Achievement Test*[15]
- *Woodcock-JohnsonPsycho-EducationalBattery-Tests of Achievement*[16]
- *Kaufman Assessment Battery for Children*[17]
- *Peabody Individual Achievement Test-Revised*[18]
- *Wide Range Achievement Test-Third Revision*[19]

Adaptive Behavior Scales. Adaptive behavior scales determine a child's ability to function independently in routine, day-to-day life skills such as eating, dressing, social skills, self-direction, and so on. This type of test is generally administered only if the child's intelligence is significantly below average. One example is the *AAMR Adaptive Behavior Scale-School-Second Revision.*[20]

Perceptual-Motor Tests. These tests determine how well the student can process (input) information visually or auditorially and then respond (output) in some way (usually by drawing, handwriting, etc.). Two of the more popular visual processing tests are the *Developmental Test of Visual-Motor Integration-Fourth Edition*[21] and the *Visual Motor Gestalt Test.*[22] Both of these tests present the student with picture cards that display various geometric shapes (e.g., a square, a cross, a circular array of dots, etc.), and the child is asked to draw the shapes on a piece of paper. An example of an auditory processing test is the *Test of Auditory Processing Skills.*[23]

Speech-Language Surveys. These tests determine whether the child is at-risk for a speech or language disorder and whether a more comprehensive evaluation from a speech-language pathologist is warranted. An example of a speech articulation screening measure is the *Secord Test of Minimal Articulation Competence.*[24] An example of a language screening measure would be the *Clinical Evaluation of Language Function-Revised.*[25]

Emotional-Behavior Rating Scales. These tests determine whether a student possesses significant problems in self-control, anxiety-depression, social interaction, psychotic behavior, conduct disorders, etc. Generally, these scales are completed by persons (e.g., parents or classroom teachers) who are thoroughly familiar with the child and can accurately assess his behavior based on prior observations. One popularly used instrument in this category is the *Revised Behavior Problem Checklist*.[26]

Attention Rating Scales. These rating scales determine whether a child has significant problems in attention, impulsivity, or hyperactivity, which may be the basis for an attention deficit disorder. Examples of this type of measure would be the *Attention Deficit Disorder Evaluation Scale*[27] and the *ADHD Rating Scale-IV*.[28]

Giftedness Rating Scales. Giftedness rating scales function much like the other types of rating scales in that they determine the likelihood that a student possesses significant giftedness and talent in a particular domain such as leadership, intelligence, specific academic aptitude, performing and visual arts, etc. The *Gifted Evaluation Scale*[29] is an example.

Diagnostic Skill Tests

There are many types of diagnostic skill tests on the market today that cover a variety of academic areas. What follows is a list of some of the more popularly administered, one-on-one diagnostic tests used by diagnosticians today.

School Readiness Skill Tests

- *Brigance Diagnostic Comprehensive Test of Basic Skills-Readiness Subtest*[30]
- *Denver II Screening*[31]

General Academic Skills Tests.

- *Brigance Diagnostic Comprehensive Inventory of Basic Skills*[32]
- *Wechsler Individual Achievement Test*[33]

Reading Skill Tests.

- *Durrell Analysis of Reading Difficulty*[34]
- *Gray Oral Reading Test-Revised*[35]
- *Stanford Diagnostic Reading Test*[36]
- *Test of Reading Comprehension:Revised Edition*[37]

Spelling/Writing Skill Tests.

- *Test of Written Spelling 2*[38]
- *Spellmaster Assessment and Teaching System*[39]
- *Test of Written Language*[40]
- *Test of Legible Handwriting*[41]

Mathematics Skill Tests.

- *KeyMath Revised: A Diagnostic Inventory of Essential Mathematics*[42]
- *Diagnostic Mathematics Inventory/Mathematics System*[43]
- *Test of Mathematical Ability*[44]

Achievement Tests

One-on-one achievement tests need to be administered to children with disabilities and other struggling learners in order to measure their academic growth and performance over a given period of time. Parents may want to have one-on-one achievement tests administered annually. One-on-one achievement tests must be administered by a qualified diagnostician. Two individually administered achievement tests are described below.

- *Wechsler Individual Achievement Test.*[45] This comprehensive battery of subtests measures the child's achievement across the reading, writing, language and mathematics domains. Specific subtests include basic reading, reading comprehension, spelling, written expression, oral expression, listening comprehension, mathematics reasoning, and numerical operations (mathematics computation).
- *Woodcock-Johnson Psycho-Educational Battery-Tests of Achievement.*[46] This one-on-one administered achievement test includes both standard and supplementary batteries covering a broad array of subtests that assess the child's achievement across the language arts, mathematics, and other academic areas. Specific subtests include letter-word identification, passage comprehension, word attack, reading vocabulary, proofing (spelling, word usage, and punctuation), dictation (spelling, word usage, punctuation, and capitalization), writing samples, writing fluency (hand-

writing), calculation, applied problems, quantitative concepts, science, social studies, and humanities.

Screening Tests

Children who are genuinely disabled (i.e., learning disabled, attention deficit disordered, etc.) must meet necessary criteria in order to be classified (see Chapter 1). The fact that there are minimal criteria for these different forms of disabilities suggests that not all children who have learning, attention, or behavior difficulties will have bonafide disabilities. Unfortunately, parents may invest hundreds of dollars in a comprehensive, in-depth psychoeducational evaluation only to discover that their child's behavior problems were not serious enough to warrant a disability classification. Parents can avoid costly testing fees by requesting that screening-type instruments be administered to the child prior to evaluation.

The concept of screening is used often in the medical field. For example, suppose a patient complains of severe pain in his lower right abdomen. A physician may initially conclude that the person's appendix needs to be removed (a screening decision). Until the patient undergoes more comprehensive health examination, however, the suspected need for an appendectomy cannot be conclusively determined. Screening procedures are also used for other health conditions such as pregnancy and serious illnesses like cancer.

Screening for a disability in educational circles is a process that is similar to screening in the medical field. Under the supervision of a diagnostician, parents are asked to rate the frequency of their child's behaviors and complete rating scale instruments of their child's problem behaviors. These screening tests, completed in the comfort of the home (i.e., the diagnostician does not have to be present), are commercially-produced tests that will generate a statistical number which compares the frequency of the child's behaviors with a norm sample of children who have been formally classified as disabled. Because these instruments include statistical scoring and analysis, the parents must return the completed rating scales to the diagnostician who scores and interprets the results for the parents. If the child's resulting rating score falls below a certain criterion, then the child is determined to be *at risk* for a disability.

Home-administered rating scales are not robust enough, nor do they include enough varied data, for a definitive decision to be made about whether or not the child has a disability. Only through a follow-up, comprehensive psychoeducational evaluation can the suspected disability be confirmed or rejected. Screening-type tests are a wise, inexpensive first step for parents who may be considering an evaluation for their child. Pre-evaluation screening results will help parents decide more confidently whether or not to invest additional dollars in follow-up testing.

Learning Style Evaluations

A number of factors can influence a child's academic success, for example, the child's mood and attitude toward his school work, the parent-child relationship, the quality of curricular materials, and so on. We also know that the instructional environment and all the variables that make up the school setting can enhance or adversely affect school success in children. Although learning, attention, and behavioral problems may signal a potential disability, these same difficulties could also indicate a mismatch between the child's preferences for learning and the way his classroom environment is arranged.

A child's learning and environmental preferences can be evaluated through commercially-produced learning style instruments. Like screening-type instruments, learning style instruments (sometimes called *inventories*) can be administered in the home by the parents under the supervision of a diagnostician. These instruments determine how much or how little a child prefers certain learning and environmental variables such as noise, light, need for structure, visual-auditory-kinesthetic-tactile learning preferences, etc.

Once the learning style instrument is completed, the parent returns it to the examiner for scoring and analysis. Findings from this type of testing allow the parent to modify the learning environment so that learning conditions will be maximized for the child. For example, if the child prefers some degree of noise in the background while doing school work, the parent could easily adapt the home learning environment by allowing the child to listen to soft music while working.

Informal Skill Assessment

In addition to screening-type tests and learning style inventories that can be administered in the home, parents can also do some diagnostic skill assessment on their own. This type of informal testing is primarily designed to assist the parent in identifying specific reading, writing, spelling, and mathematics skills that the child may not have mastered which are expected of typical students in the child's corresponding chronological grade. Ideally, the parent should collaborate with a diagnostician who would be able to administer diagnostic tests on a one-on-one basis. But, as we have noted earlier, the expense factor may prevent some families from being able to secure professional testing.

Nonetheless, if parents are to remediate academic skill deficits in their children, they will need to know the specific skills the child has not mastered. In order for parents to develop and conduct an informal diagnostic assessment in the home, we suggest following steps:

1. Locate a scope and sequence skills list for the child's current grade placement and all prior grade levels in the subject area of concern (many curriculum manuals provide such lists; the book entitled, *Teaching Students with Learning Problems*[47] also contains skills lists);
2. Develop at least three test items that reflect each specific skill on the list;
3. Administer the items for the different skills to the child (gradually over the course of several weeks);
4. Plan remediation lessons for each specific skill in which the child was unable to demonstrate 100% mastery (i.e., 3 out of 3 correct items).

At the time of this publication, we are completing the development of a diagnostic mathematics skill test that parents will be able to administer and score in the home. The test will be published by *Exceptional Diagnostics*, the testing service operated by your authors (see Appendix A for our mailing address).

Qualifications of Diagnosticians

Parents would certainly expect their family physician to have high credentials and extensive preparation in the medical field, particularly if their child needed surgery for a serious illness. Similarly, parents will want to employ professionals who are properly qualified and prepared to administer individual educational tests. Some one-on-one achievement and diagnostic skill tests may be administered by teachers who hold bachelor's degrees in special education or other educators who hold master's degrees. But virtually all other individual educational tests should be administered by qualified diagnosticians. Psychoeducational evaluations in particular should be conducted by licensed professionals.[48]

Qualified diagnosticians are plentiful in many parts of the country. You will see greater numbers near larger cities. A perusal of our telephone directory in the Greenville, SC area yielded a count of over fifty psychologists, psychiatrists, psychotherapists, psychoanalysts, counselors, and hypnotherapists, all vying for a piece of the client testing pool. When the field of possible candidates has the potential to be this large, parents must exercise wisdom in choosing the right diagnostician. We believe the following characteristics describe the ideal diagnostician for Christian parents.

1. A Bible-believing Christian. The field of special education assessment, like most other aspects of public education, reeks with secular humanistic philosophy and practices. Typical diagnosticians today (e.g., psychologists, psychiatrists, etc.) believe in treatments and make recommendations that reflect their secular humanistic beliefs that more often than not run counter to Truth. Many of these professionals accept the premise that the child is not ultimately responsible and accountable for his behavior. A Christian diagnostician will embrace Biblical values and filter all recommendations in the light of God's Word. Unfortunately, very few diagnosticians are Christian. Parents can dispel doubt by simply asking the diagnostician up front if he is a Christian prior to making an appointment.

2. Home school friendly. Our experience has been that many, if not most, professional diagnosticians are strong advocates of public education. We have personally read test reports from some secular diagnosticians who literally chastised parents for choosing to teach their children at home. Clearly, parents will want to employ an examiner who is amiable toward their efforts of home education. Once parents have exhausted their own personal searches and still come up empty-handed, consider making contact with the following organizations for recommendations:

- Home School Legal Defense Association's Special Education Department (See Appendix A);
- NATHHAN (National Challenged Homeschoolers Associated Network See Appendix A);
- Individual state home school organizations (A list can be provided by contacting The Teaching Home See Appendix A); and
- Local home school support groups.

3. Holds an advanced degree. Parents will want professionals who have a minimum of a master's degree (e.g., M.A., M.S., or M.Ed.) or earned doctorate (e.g., Ph.D. or Ed.D.) in school psychology, psychometry, special education, or other related field. A graduate degree signifies that the diagnostician has studied assessment and identification procedures thoroughly and is equipped to recommend effective educational interventions that parents can implement in the home.

4. Holds a license or certificate. Qualified diagnosticians should hold a license or certificate from a national, regional, or state certifying board. For example, most school psychologists are licensed by departments of education in their respective states. Others may hold licenses from a national board (e.g., National Association of Certified School Psychologists). Although not as common now, there are a few states who still license educational diagnosticians. In addition to their testing skills, these professionals generally have backgrounds in the field of special education and extensive classroom teaching experience with disabled students.

5. Holds memberships in professional organizations. Memberships in professional organizations (e.g., Council for Exceptional Children, Council for Educational Diagnostic Services, National Council for Educational Measurement, American Psychological Association) offer some evidence that the diagnostician is receiving continuing education and preparation in the field of assessment. Most of these professional organizations will publish journals and periodicals that disseminate current research, practices, and policies on how students should be evaluated.

Free Public School Testing

Local public schools, under federal mandates from Public Law 101-476, the Individuals with Disabilities Education Act, must provide free testing to all referred children, whether or not they are currently enrolled in that public school. This provision of the law extends to all private and home school students. But we strongly urge parents to steer clear of this free testing for a number of reasons.

One, the confidentiality that most parents covet may be violated since public school officials will have access to the child's scores after the assessment is completed. This is especially true if parents continue home education and do not enroll the child in a public school program. Two, the public school psychologist will in all likelihood not be a Christian, which means that the parent will have to endure secular, humanistic recommendations and treatment or service options for the child, which, as we mentioned earlier, will surely run counter to our Christian values and faith.

Three, since they are investing in the life of the child to some degree through free assessment, public school officials will probably feel some sense of ownership of the child. Assuming the child is eventually classified as disabled, the parents consequently may have to endure undue pressure from public educators with regard to enrolling the child in their special education programs. While it may be awfully tempting, home educators are cautioned not to receive any special education or related services (e.g., speech-language therapy, physical therapy, etc.) from the public schools. Parents may be in danger of *legal entanglement*, if litigation ensues later. (Contact HSLDA for information regarding the entanglement issue.)

Given these three major limitations, we recommend that parents, particularly those who are full-time home educators, employ *private* diagnosticians for all their testing needs. To take advantage of free testing services from the public schools may be financially convenient for the moment, but it may mean having to "pay the piper" (i.e., the public school system) down the road.

Time Line for Testing

Determining when a student should be tested is based in part on the type of testing. For example, once an initial psychoeducational evaluation has been conducted and the child is classified as disabled, the consensus of professional opinion is that the child should be re-evaluated every three years until he graduates from high school. Special educators refer to this as a *triennial evaluation*. Triennial evaluations are required by law (Public Law 101-476) for students with disabilities who are enrolled in public schools.

We believe that triennial evaluations are necessary for home educated students with disabilities for two reasons. One is that parents will want to determine periodically if there has been any change in their child's abilities and achievement. Results from subsequent evaluations may mean that the child's original classification needs to be changed (e.g., from ADD to LD) or removing the original label altogether. A second reason is that a triennial evaluation may indicate that an adjustment in the child's educational program needs to be made. For example, a child's learning disability in mathematics computation may have worsened, which would suggest that more intensive special education is needed.

Parents may desire to have diagnostic skill evaluations done more frequently, for example, every other year, particularly if the parent is using diagnostic test results as a basis for planning remedial instruction or perhaps in developing an individual education plan (see Chapter 4). If the parents want even more frequent documentation of the child's annual progress, an annual diagnostic evaluation may be desired. Whether or not the parent chooses an annual diagnostic evaluation, one-on-one achievement tests should be done annually.

We believe the frequency with which struggling learners receive individual educational testing should be guided by several important considerations:

1. State home school laws may have special testing requirements. States vary in their testing requirements. Some may have more rigorous testing requirements than others for students with documented disabilities. Pennsylvania, for example, requires that all children educated at home in grades three, five, and eight take "nationally normed standardized achievement tests in reading/language arts and mathematics..."[49] We suggest that our readers consult with the Home School Legal Defense Association for information on individual state testing requirements.

2. Court litigation requires careful documentation of child progress. The volatility of the field of special education combined with the ever increasing media attention toward minorities, suggests that home educators who teach students with disabilities at home *may* be more at risk for government intrusion and impending litigation. Therefore, regular testing and evaluation for purposes of documentation is not only the wise order of the day, but it may be the parents' best defense. Somerville, a senior attorney with the Home School Legal Defense Association, offers this advice:

> With so much of the [special education] law unclear, it is critical to focus on the facts in any court case. Home-schooling works for children with special needs. If we can put an expert witness on the stand to testify that the family is doing a good job and getting good results, we can win. If we can't, we are likely to lose, no matter what the law says.[50]

Implicit in Somerville's position is that the expert witness has little with which to testify on behalf of the parents' effectiveness without empirical evidence (i.e., formal test results). Clearly, a more compelling case could be made that parents are getting good results from home instruction if parents are scheduling periodic evaluations for the child.

Our experience as special educators has been that proving the effectiveness of teaching disabled students hinges primarily on progress that can be documented through regular testing and evaluation. While increasing attention is being given to the portfolio assessment concept (i.e., gathering samples of the child's school work products) for documenting progress, parents who have children with disabilities may not want to document progress solely on portfolio material. No doubt, if litigation ensues, the court will likely ask for formal test data on the child as evidence of a parent's effort to educate the child properly in the home.

We strongly recommend that parents who are full-time home educators consider joining the Home School Legal Defense Association. HSLDA attorneys will be able to provide member parents with individualized legal advice with regard to seeking professional testing, while taking into account the family's financial resources and the peculiarities of the parents' respective state home school laws.

3. Effectiveness hinges on evidence that the child is improving. Results from individual testing speak to the effectiveness of your home education efforts and whether or not you are successfully remediating learning, attention, and behavior difficulties in your struggling learner. More frequent testing will allow parents to make adjustments in the child's home program quickly without losing significant instructional time.

The Cost Factor

Like many other services in our lives where professionals are involved (e.g., mechanics, electricians, computer specialists), the costs for individual educational testing can be expensive. Fees can range from a few hundred to a thousand or more dollars, depending on the part of the country you reside and the professional credentials and experience the diagnostician holds. For example, testing fees for diagnosticians who live near larger, metropolitan cities may be more than those who live in rural areas. Those who hold doctorates (e.g., Ph.D. or Ed.D.) may charge higher fees than those who have master's degrees.

For parents who are financially strapped, securing needed professional testing may seem impossible, but the following options should provide hope:

- Negotiate with the diagnostician regarding the possibility of allowing you to pay the test fee in interest-free installments.
- Seek the financial assistance of grandparents, who may recognize the significance of having their grandchild evaluated.
- Check with agencies and organizations (e.g., Ch.A.D.D. and NATHHAN) that are advocates of children with disabilities to see if they have grant monies available for testing.
- Make advanced contact with your health insurance agent to see if psychological or psychoeducational testing is covered in your plan.
- Begin setting aside and saving a little money each month and plan ahead to have testing done in the near future.[51]

Justifying the cost factor requires that parents fully understand the impact of both money and time. Coming up with the money to pay for individual testing will surely require great sacrifice for most parents. But the financial sting is not permanent since money can be regained over the course of time. When parents repeatedly defer individual testing, however, something much more important than money is forfeited that can never be recaptured—time. The early years when young children can be remediated more effectively come around only once. Parents should make every effort to secure individual testing and evaluation early on so that disabilities can be identified and tailor-made programs can be developed to meet the child's needs.

---

[1]J. Sutton (1993b)
[2]Vergason (1990)
[3]Stephens (1977)
[4]Salvia & Ysseldyke (1995)
[5]Brigance (1983)
[6]Woodcock & Johnson (1989a)
[7]Connolly (1988)
[8]Psychological Corporation (1992a)
[9]Luftig (1987), p. 60
[10]Psychological Corporation (1991)
[11]Thorndike, Hagen, & Sattler (1995)
[12]Woodcock & Johnson (1989b)
[13]A. Kaufman & N. Kaufman (1983)
[14]Hammill (1991)
[15]Psychological Corporation (1992b)
[16]Woodcock & Johnson (1989a)
[17]A. Kaufman & N. Kaufman (1983)
[18]Markwardt (1989)
[19]Wilkinson (1993)
[20]Lambert, Nihira, & Leland (1993)
[21]Beery (1997)
[22]Bender (1938)
[23]Gardner (1985)
[24]Secord (1981)
[25]Semel, Wiig, & Secord (1989)
[26]Quay & Peterson (1983)
[27]McCarney (1989)
[28]DuPaul, Anastopoulos, Power, Murphy, & Barkley (1996)
[29]McCarney (1987)
[30]Brigance (1983)
[31]Frankenburg, Dodds, Archer, Bresnick, Maschaa, Edelman, & Shapiro (1990)
[32]Brigance (1983)
[33]Psychological Corporation (1992b)
[34]Durrell & Catterson (1980)
[35]Wiederholt & Bryant (1992)
[36]Karlsen & Gardner (1985)
[37]Brown, Hammill, & Wiederholt (1986)
[38]Larsen & Hammill (1986)
[39]Greenbaum (1987)
[40]Hammill & Larsen (1988)
[41]Larsen & Hammill (1989)

[42]Connolly (1988)
[43]Gessell (1983)
[44]Brown & McEntire (1984)
[45]Psychological Corporation (1992b)
[46]Woodcock & Johnson (1989a)
[47]C. Mercer & A. Mercer (1993)
[48]Salvia & Ysseldyke (1991)
[49]Pennsylvania Act 169, cited in H. Richman & S. Richman (1993)
[50]Somerville (1994), p. 1
[51]J. Sutton (1994c)

4

Developing Curriculum

A sk virtually any parent what curriculum means, and you'll get answers like textbooks, workbooks, teacher manuals, manipulatives, and so on. Little wonder that curriculum is commonly perceived this way. One of the highlights of many home school conventions today is the curriculum fairs that display and sell an almost endless selection of textbooks and related materials. But curriculum entails more than just textbooks and workbooks.

Traditionally defined, curriculum means a standard course of study for all students. More recently, curriculum has come to mean, "the selection and organization of content and learning experiences."[1] Practically speaking, a curriculum is a carefully sequenced set of skills reflecting the different academic, behavioral, social, and spiritual areas that children are expected to master. The breadth and depth of these skills vary according to the chronological age and grade level of the child. Textbooks and other educational materials simply embody the many curricular skills that children are to learn. But *learning experiences* are not limited to just textbooks and workbooks alone. They may also include such activities as structured field trips and laboratory experiments.

Unfortunately, equating educational materials with curriculum may be a necessary evil that we all have to live with for the time being. It is important that parents understand, though, that "one size does not fit all" when it comes to selecting instructional materials that will eventually become part of their child's home curriculum, particularly if the child has a bona fide disability. Yet with all the hoopla and frenzy that surrounds curriculum fairs these days, it is easy for a parent to "shop till you drop" and end up with little more than a bag full of instructional materials that are totally inappropriate for a child with a disability.

It is interesting to note the sales pitches that some curriculum vendors use to try to convince a parent that their line of textbooks is the best or better than those of another publishing house. The truth is, each commercially-produced educational product, whether a textbook, workbook, or other, has its own unique set of advantages and disadvantages. For example, one set of materials may rely heavily on the child's rote memory, while another emphasizes critical thinking, yet still another may require keen long-term memory and retrieval skills in order for the child to do well, all of which can be weaknesses with disabled students.

One of the most important things to understand about many curricula on the market today is that they were designed and written for typical, average learners, not for students with disabilities.[2] The authors assume that average students will be able to master fairly quickly the scope and sequence of skills and lessons presented in their textbooks. At worst, some of the lessons in these books may need to be repeated or reviewed from time to time in order for average learners to grasp them.

But for disabled students, it's not that easy. Their learning gaps and processing difficulties many times prevent them from being able to learn successfully from typical textbooks. Debbie Mills, a home educating mother of a child with a disability, rightly states that, "For many children with disabilities the traditional scope and sequence do not apply."[3]

So, what are parents to do? A canned curriculum for struggling learners, or better yet, one of those success-oriented books for parents with struggling learners, would work! Unfortunately, there are no effective, research-proven canned curricula that we could recommend to parents. Moreover, we caution parents not to be fooled by any book that boasts an easy approach to teaching struggling learners.

Books about how to be successful at just about anything abound today. Some of these books may be valid. Others are simply sham. The danger is that many well-meaning people fall prey to the grandiose, unfounded ideas promoted in some books. More important, we believe a common message that permeates many of these success-oriented books. The message, although subtle at times, is simple— *You can obtain a lot in this life with little or no effort.* How beguiling and injurious this message is. Unfortunately, this "quick and easy...get something for nothing" philosophy has ruined many families in modern America. In truth, very few things of great value in this life can be obtained without immense effort and hard work.

So it is with teaching struggling learners. We would do our readers a great disservice if we were to suggest that teaching these children is an easy task, whether in conventional or home schools. It is not. It stands to reason that struggling learners, particularly those with disabilities, are complex individuals with very unique needs. Instruction designed to meet their needs may be as complex and involved as the children themselves.[4] Susan Parrish, a home educating mother, concluded, "I learned over time, [that] schooling an impaired child can take three times the energy, patience and knowledge and is not for the faint of heart."[5] While there are no easy answers to the curriculum question, we believe nonetheless that parents can learn how to develop programs for struggling learners, if they are willing to invest the necessary time and effort to prepare properly.

Trying to make standard curricular materials designed for typical, average learners work for struggling learners is like forcing a square peg into a round hole. One mother of two exceptional children (i.e., one with a developmental disability, the other gifted) described her frustration with standard curricula this way: "We are indoctrinated that we must have approved professional curriculum when there are probably more differences in our children's learning than literature available."[6]

Leaning totally on standard, canned curricula, then, as the primary vehicle of instruction for teaching struggling learners generally produces only frustration for both parent and child. Using a single, pre-packaged curriculum may be enough for average students, but it will most likely be insufficient for struggling learners. Although there are some very good curricula on the market today, curricular materials alone will not meet all the unique needs that struggling learners have. In short, standard curricula are simply not enough.[7] Parents must do more in the area of developing *tailor-made programs* if these children are to succeed and reach their God-given potentials.

A Good Approach

Time or financial constraints may prevent some parents from tailor-making an ideal, comprehensive, totally individualized home program for their child. Therefore, a good approach to curriculum for a struggling learner, one that we term the *modified regular curriculum approach*,[8] includes adopting one complete line of standard curriculum or a combination of subject area materials from several different standard curricula and supplementing with instructional modifications and accommodations. Modifications will be necessary in order to make the curriculum more cognitively palatable for the struggling learner. Several ideas on how to modify follow:

- Use highlighter pens, particularly the bright flamboyant colored ones to accentuate instructions, key words and phrases, etc. in textbooks and workbooks.
- Make copies of math textbook pages that contain monotonous rows of math problems and cut them into fewer, more reasonable and manageable, and less intimidating sets of problems.
- Audiotape pages in science, history, and Bible books that may be beyond the reading level of your child and allow her to listen with headphones while she follows the text visually (see Chapter 6 for complete instructions on how to audiotape textbook readings).
- Develop strategies or step-by-step checklists that will guide the child on how to complete assignments or solve problems in textbook lessons.

Parents will need to select grade level books and materials that are on the child's *functioning level* (see Chapter 3), not chronological grade level. This should allow her to move forward at a more successful pace. Parents who adopt this approach to developing curriculum should be generous in their application of modifications, accommodtions, and adaptations. We refer our readers to Chapter 6 for more ideas on how to modify instruction.

With the many different standard curricula available today, choosing one can be difficult. Parents of struggling learners may be interested in a resource by Mike and Cathy Duffy entitled, *Christian Home Educators' Curriculum Manual: Elementary Grades*[9] which provides advice on buying curricula. We are also highly impressed with a new approach to regular curriculum developed by Dr. Ron and Inge Cannon called, *Education PLUS® Curriculum*. The Cannons' curriculum is distinguished from other popular published programs available today in that it is an interdisciplinary approach to learning and places Scripture at the core of educational programming, "rather than being added on as a tangent."[10] See Appendix A for mailing addresses for more information about the Duffys' resource and the Cannons' curriculum.

A Better Approach

The major drawback of the modified regular instruction approach for struggling learners is that, at best, it only minimizes the frustration factor and maximizes the child's chances of learning more successfully in materials that were never designed for him in the first place. The child's learning gaps are ever present, though, and in all likelihood will prevent him from learning more advanced, age-appropriate material.

We believe that a *tailor-made* curriculum is a better approach over the modified regular curriculum approach. Tailor-made programs include a balance of two major strands of instruction— *remedial* and *regular* instruction. Remedial instruction is a necessary component in a tailor-made program because we know that most children who struggle, particularly those with disabilities, will have learning deficits (or learning gaps) in one or more of four basic academic areas—reading, writing, spelling, or mathematics. Parents, therefore, will need to provide daily periods of remediation in order to close the learning gaps and give children opportunities to master basic skills once and for all so that more complex material can be learned at faster rates.

Remedial instruction basically includes two steps. One, identify the specific *skills* that the child has not mastered. Two, use more intensive teaching *methods* to teach these skills. Identifying deficit skills will require some form of diagnostic testing, either formal or informal (see Chapter 3). Knowing which methods to use to teach those skills will call for parents to study and learn about the different teaching techniques that can be incorporated in remedial instruction (see Chapters 7, 8, and 9).

Remedial instruction alone, though, is not enough for struggling learners either. Many of these children, even those with disabilities, have intelligence that is well within the average range, which suggests that they also have the ability to learn from regular curricular materials, as long as it is on their functioning level. A key to effective tailor-made programs is integrating regular instruction with remedial instruction. It is critically important that parents keep struggling learners on a regular course of instruction, at their functioning level, so they can progress in a normal scope and sequence of instruction that is expected of typical learners.

Not all skills presented in regular curricular materials require that the child master all of his skill deficits in advance. This means that the student is capable of learning some skills as presented in regular textbooks and workbooks, without pausing to go back and learn (or relearn) prerequisite skills. For example, learning geometric concepts in math, some quite elevated, do not rely heavily on complete mastery of computational skills (i.e., addition, subtraction, multiplication, and division).

So, more appropriate tailor-made programs for struggling learners will include a balance of regular and remedial instruction. For students with more severe skill deficits, parents may choose to allocate more daily instructional time to remedial than regular instruction. Children with more mild learning difficulties can survive and improve with less remedial time each day. The beauty of teaching children in the home is that parents have complete charge of modifying the learning program (i.e., more time for this, less time for that) and can make changes immediately in daily allocations of instructional time as they see a need.

Individualized Educational Plan

Most of us can testify that we have at least once in our lives observed a building that was the result of faulty planning. Perhaps the builder had not anticipated the costs involved and ran out of money. Or perhaps he decided to take the plan-as-you-go route, resulting in a mass of piecemeal designs that lacked unity and had structural problems. Whatever the reason, the lack of planning is obvious to all who pass by, and the time and money spent were not well invested. On the other hand, adequately planned structures are structurally sound, functional in layout, and pleasing to the eye. The time and money invested in the blueprint will pay off when the builder carries out the plan.

The task of educating a learner with limitations is monumental. Developing a tailor-made curriculum goes a long way in simplifying the task. However, parents can simplify the task even more if they develop a carefully constructed written plan or blueprint of instruction. Special educators refer to such a plan as the *individualized education plan* (IEP). In essence, the IEP documents the level at which the child is currently functioning and the academic and behavioral goals and objectives for a specific period, usually a school year.

Federal Law requires an IEP for students receiving special education services within the public school system. Legislators intended to insure that students removed from regular classrooms, either all or some of the school day, would receive meaningful instruction tailored to meet their individual needs. So if the IEP is a legal requirement for public school special educators, do homeschooling parents of children with disabilities need to write IEP's? Although parents may not be bound legally to have an IEP on the child, there are several good reasons for having one.

The primary purpose for an IEP is planning. Without a carefully formulated plan, the teacher may wander aimlessly from one material or approach to another. Debbie Mills, home educating mother of a disabled child, says that, "When there are no text books to work through, the I.E.P. becomes the curriculum."[11]

Another important reason for writing an IEP is documentation. If someone should question whether a child educated in the home were receiving an appropriate education, the IEP documents the plans that will meet the child's specific needs. As parents carry out the IEP, it then provides documentation of goals and objectives that the student has met. Somerville, of the Home School Legal Defense Association, believes that, "even though IEP's are not necessary for homeschooling families, good documentation is still a must."[12] This documentation may prove to be valuable in case of a legal challenge.

Elements of an IEP

So, what does writing an IEP involve?   Based on instructions contained in Public Laws 94-142 and 101-476, the required elements of an IEP for public educators include the following:

- present level of educational performance
- annual goals
- short-term instructional objectives
- evaluation criteria
- type and amount of special education and related services
- extent of inclusion with nondisabled students
- transitions plans and services for adolescents
- beginning and ending dates of the program

Once more, formal IEP's are *not* required of those who are educating children outside the realm of public, federally-funded schools, which would include home schools. If a home education program ever comes under legal challenge, however, it will be more credible if parents have an IEP that follows the pattern established by federal law. We believe that parents are capable of developing their own IEP's, although some may choose to get assistance from a special education consultant. In the paragraphs below, we provide an explanation of each IEP element.

Present Level of Educational Performance

The present level of educational performance, written in paragraph form, describes the strengths and weaknesses of the child academically. It may also include social and emotional-behavioral characteristics. In addition to describing the extent of a child's cognitive abilities (i.e., his learning potential), this section of the IEP will probably include statements describing his math and reading levels, abilities in oral and written expression, and progress in the content areas. The summary may include the child's learning and modality preferences (i.e., visual, auditory, kinesthetic, and/or tactile). This information may be pulled from a variety of sources including psycho–educational evaluations, diagnostic evaluations, recent achievement tests, and parent-teacher observations.

Annual Goals

The summary of the present level of performance is a springboard for annual goals and short term objectives. The child's present abilities help determine his goals in each area of need for the coming year. For example, a child's IEP may contain annual goal statements in the major academic areas such as reading, spelling, and mathematics. But a child's IEP could also contain an annual goal statement in other areas such as adaptive behavior (if the child is developmentally disabled). Whatever the case, the number of annual goal statements will vary from one child to the next, depending on the specific areas of need. A child may have significant spiritual needs that should be addressed and for which an annual goal should be stated on the IEP. We refer our readers to an IEP approach that emphasizes the teaching of Biblical concepts in a book on Christian special education entitled, *Special Education: A Biblical Approach*.[13]

Each goal statement should describe what the child should be able to accomplish by the end of the year. In short, the annual goal is simply an instructional target. It is an indication of where the parent expects the child to be, educationally speaking, at the end of the program period. A typical mathematics goal statement for a student with a mild disability and currently achieving at a grade equivalent of 4.0 in mathematics might be, "Tommy will earn a grade score of 5.0 in numerical operations on the *Wechsler Individual Achievement Test* by June, 1995."

Short-term Instructional Objectives

Short-term objectives are the instructional steps that ultimately lead to accomplishment of an annual goal. Parents may need to spend several weeks addressing one instructional objective with a child by presenting and teaching the skill from different instructional angles. By completing all short-term objectives in a given area, the student will have met his annual goal. Parents will need to formulate anywhere from five to ten instructional objectives per goal statement. An example of a typical short-term objective that leads to Tommy's mathematics goal might be, "Given a set of ten problems presented via computer, Tommy will be able to add two-digit numbers with regrouping at 90% accuracy."

The goals and objectives contained on a student's IEP address the areas in which the student has learning deficits, which in essence will serve as part of the *remediation* component of the child's tailor-made curriculum. For example, if the student is functioning at expected age or grade level in spelling, then IEP goals and objectives in spelling are not necessary since the student will be following the scope and sequence of skills in a regular curriculum. In order to identify the specific skills in which a child has deficits, the parent will have to have some type of diagnostic skill testing done, either formal or informal (see Chapter 3).

Criteria for Evaluation

Next, the IEP must show plans for evaluation of these objectives. The plan should show *how* the parent plans to evaluate the student's performance (e.g., parent-made test, commercially produced test, timed test, flashcards, oral questioning, parent observation, etc.) for stated objectives and *what level* of mastery the student must attain (e.g., 90% accuracy, 50 correct responses in 3 minutes, etc.). With the child's abilities and potential in mind, the level of mastery is chosen by the parent. However, the mastery level may be stipulated by Department of Education in the state that the parent resides. Parents who are members of the Home School Legal Defense Association should consult their state's attorney regarding this matter.

Special Education and Related Services

A statement of specific educational services lists *what* areas need remediation (or special education), the types of related services (such as speech or physical therapy), *who* will provide each of the services, *where* the service will take place, and *when* and *how long* the service will be delivered.

Extent of Inclusion with Nondisabled

Students with disabilities need opportunities where they may mingle, play, and interact with other nondisabled children so that they can transfer what they are learning in the home, particularly social aspects of learning (e.g., getting along with others). The IEP should include times when the child will be involved with other children outside the one-on-one, highly individualized home teaching environment. For example, a parent may teach a daily group lesson to all of her children in such areas as Bible or social studies. The child may attend a weekly group science, music, or art lesson at a neighbor's house, a weekly group physical education activity at the YMCA, or take monthly field trips with other children. These should be listed as specifically as possible on the IEP.

Transition Services

Moving from high school to the world of work or college (typically referred to as *transition*) is difficult enough for students who do not struggle, but for children with disabilities it can be an extremely traumatic time. This transition requirement was only recently mandated by Public Law 101-476 and has been added to the original list of seven IEP elements that were specified in Public Law 94-142.

The intent of the transition services provision is to stipulate the plans on how the student will be transitioned. For example, parents may specify that part of the student's educational program during his junior and senior year would include a job training or internship position with an employer in the community, where the student would be able to learn and apply specific job skills. Salvia and Ysseldyke[14] indicate that federal special education law requires transitional services for students when they reach the age of sixteen.

Beginning and Ending Dates

Finally, the IEP must also include the dates that services are expected to begin and the proposed date of completion. Most IEP's also include projected dates for beginning each of the objectives with space to document completion of objectives. Additionally, some IEP's specify what special methods or materials will be used to accomplish each objective. For example, a parent may indicate on the IEP that the Fernald's multisensory-VAKT method (see Chapter 7) and a computer software program will be used to teach an objective that calls for a child to learn his 0-3 multiplication facts.

Are IEP goals and objectives written in stone? Even the most carefully made plans may need some adjustment from time to time during the course of a school year. Parents may find their expectations were too high (the student did not reach the goal this year) or too low (the student reached it before the year was over). If the parent discovers early on that a particular goal was quite unrealistic, he may amend it during the school year.

The intent of the federal law is to allow some degree of flexibility in adjusting the student's IEP goals and objectives. Public educators are not held accountable if the goals are not met as long as a good faith effort is made in trying to achieve them. Again, parents should probably check with their respective states (or the HSLDA) to determine for sure how much flexibility they have in making adjustments.

Formats for IEP's vary widely; however, they all should contain the same required basic elements. Developing an IEP will involve time and careful consideration, and, as we indicated earlier, may require some degree of professional assessment, if the parent does not intend to conduct informal diagnostic assessment in the home. However, the time and effort invested should result in a blueprint of instruction that is geared to the child's unique needs. Moreover, developing and implementing an IEP is one way to ensure that remediation is being provided for the child in the tailor-made curriculum.

We have chosen for illustration purposes an IEP that one home educating father and mother used for their son who has spina bifida (see Figure 4.1). Please note that assistance in developing this IEP was provided by a special education consultant.

---

[1]Armstrong, Henson, & Savage (1993)
[2]J. Sutton (1995)
[3]Mills (1995)
[4]J. Sutton (1996a)
[5]Parrish (1995), p. 42
[6]Personal communication with authors, February 6, 1995
[7]J. Sutton (1994a)
[8]J. Sutton (1995)
[9]M. Duffy & C. Duffy (1997)
[10]R. Cannon & I. Cannon (1996)
[11]Mills (1995), p. 20
[12]Somerville (1994), p. 1
[13]J. Sutton (1993c)
[14]Salvia & Ysseldye (1995)

Figure 4.1

Individualized Educational Plan

STUDENT: Brian Scott Davis

DISABILITY: PD

AGE: 12 yrs. 3 mos.

GRADE: 5.0

SCHOOL: Davis Home School

SCHOOL YEAR: 1994-95

PARENTS: David & Jennifer Davis

CONSULTANT: John P. Doe

ADDRESS: RD 3 Box 577-B, Anytown, USA

PHONE: 999-999-9999

RELATED SERVICES: Physical therapy

DATE WRITTEN: 9-28-94

CURRENT LEVEL OF PERFORMANCE:

Brian's most recent psychoeducational evaluation conducted in 1990 assessed his intelligence to be subaverage on the K-ABC test. However, in 1989, Brian's verbal IQ was determined to be low average on the WISC-R. From the diagnostic educational evaluation conducted by this consultant on 6-13-94, Brian's current grade scores on the WIAT achievement test across the academic subject areas were as follows:

Basic Reading	5.1	*	Mathematics Reasoning	K.8
Spelling	2.8		Reading Comprehension	2.9
Numerical Operations	1.4		Listening Comprehension	1.3
Oral Expression	2.4		Written Expression	2.1

STRENGTHS AND WEAKNESSES:

Although God has been pleased to allow Brian to have spina bifida, which disables him both physically and academically, Brian possesses a number of strengths that allow him to compensate for those weaknesses. For example, Brian has excellent social skills. He is able to establish and maintain excellent positive relationships with people, both young and old. Brian also has unusually good communication skills. His ability to verbalize well should serve him well as he progresses through school, as he has difficulties in his written communication skills.

BEHAVIORAL OBSERVATIONS:

Brian exhibits very good self-control of behavior. He responds well to authority. He presents himself to be a young boy of unusual maturity. He knows when to ask for help and is not embarrassed doing so.

INITIATION-TERMINATION OF SERVICE:

Brian's special education services will be delivered one-on-one by his parents and will begin the present year at the signing of this document and terminates June 30, 1995.

EXTENT OF SPECIAL EDUCATION SERVICES:

Subject	Time/Daily	Location	Teacher
Reading	20 min.	Home	Mrs. Davis
Spelling	20 min.	Home	Mrs. Davis
Written Expression	30 min.	Home	Mrs. Davis
Mathematics	30 min.	Home	Mrs. Davis

Brian will receive instruction in the other subject areas (e.g., heritage studies, science, Bible, etc.) from standard curricula with modifications and accommodations as needed. Every attempt will be made to use curricula in these areas that reflect his current grade placement.

EXTENT OF MAINSTREAMING EFFORTS:

Since Brian's home special education program represents a unique educational setting that is highly individualized (i.e., parent and student), mainstreaming efforts will obviously be limited compared to students educated in conventional school settings. Nonetheless, Mrs. Davis recognizes the necessity of giving Brian opportunities to be integrated with other nondisabled individuals in order for him to be able to transfer what he is learning to broader contexts. Thus, the following activities have been planned to address this need:

Activity	Time/Week	Supervisor
Piano lessons	30 minutes	Miss Jennifer Cook
Sunday School/Church	3-4 hours	Mr. John Smith
Children's Choir	1 hour, 30 minutes	Mrs. Debbie Jones
Community soccer games	1 hour	Mr. and Mrs. Davis
Community basketball games	1 hour	Mr. and Mrs. Davis
Chapel with Christian school	45 minutes	Mrs. Davis

TRANSITION SERVICES:

Disabled students who are in their high school years and approaching graduation from high school need transition services. The purpose of a transition plan is to allow for smooth entry of the young adult into the community/job world, if the student is not anticipating post-secondary education. Yet for those disabled young people who are planning on furthering their education (e.g., community/technical college or baccalaureate, four-year college degree program), a plan still needs to be developed to help them bridge their exit from high school to the college setting. No transition plan is needed for Brian at this time.

READING

ANNUAL GOAL: Brian will improve his overall reading achievement to a grade
score of 6.0 on the WIAT achievement test by June, 1995.

	TYPE EVALUATION:	DATE COMPLETED:
INSTRUCTIONAL OBJECTIVE:		
1. Brian will be able to read age-appropriate words with short vowel sounds "i" and "o" with 100% accuracy.	_____	_____
2. Brian will be able to read age-appropriate words with long vowel sounds "e", "i", and "u" with 100% accuracy.	_____	_____
3. Brian will be able to read and pronounce age-appropriate words with proper syllabication and accent with 100% accuracy.	_____	_____
4. Brian will be able to answer questions from reading passages that have to do with recognizing stated cause and effect with at least 90% accuracy.	_____	_____
5. Brian will be able to answer questions from reading passages that have to do with comparing and contrasting with at least 90% accuracy.	_____	_____
6. Brian will be able to answer questions from reading passages that have to do with predicting events and outcomes with at least 90% accuracy.	_____	_____
7. Brian will be able to answer questions from reading passages that have to do with recognizing stated detail with at least 90% accuracy.	_____	_____

Evaluation Codes: OQ=oral questions; TT=teacher-made test; CT=commercially-
made test; TO=teacher observation.

SPELLING

ANNUAL GOAL: Brian will improve his spelling achievement to a grade score of 5.0 on the WIAT achievement test by June, 1995.

INSTRUCTIONAL OBJECTIVE:	TYPE EVALUATION:	DATE COMPLETED:
1. Brian will be able to spell words with the following suffixes with at least 90% accuracy: -n,-less,-vies,-or,-ous,-ance, -ant,-ence,-ible,-ian,-ation,-ity,-ize	____	____
2. Brian will be able to spell words with the following prefixes with at least 90% accuracy: de-,en-,ir-,anti-,semi-	____	____
3. Brian will be able to spell all of the days of the week with at least 100% accuracy.	____	____
4. Brian will be able to spell all of the months of the year with at least 100% accuracy.	____	____
5. Brian will be able to spell homophone words (e.g., write/right; eight/ate, etc.) with at least 90% accuracy.	____	____

Evaluation Codes: OQ=oral questions; TT=teacher-made test; CT=commercially-made test; TO=teacher observation.

WRITTEN EXPRESSION

ANNUAL GOAL: Brian will improve his overall writing achievement to a grade score of 5.0 on the WIAT achievement test by June, 1995.

INSTRUCTIONAL OBJECTIVE:	TYPE EVALUATION:	DATE COMPLETED:
1. Brian will be able to take a topic of interest and generate three main points and several subpoints with at least 100% accuracy.	____	____
2. Brian will be able to write complete sentences including subject, verb, and direct object with 100% accuracy.	____	____
3. Brian will be able to capitalize words in sentences that represent groups of people (e.g., Campfire Girls, Boy Scouts, etc.) with 100% accuracy.	____	____
4. Brian will be able to capitalize words in sentences that represent government groups, business firms, and product brand names with 100% accuracy.	____	____
5. Brian will be able to place a comma between city and state in sentences with 100% accuracy.	____	____
6. Brian will be able to place periods after initials in names in sentences with 100% accuracy.	____	____
7. Brian will be able to place apostrophes for possessive nouns in sentences with 100% accuracy.	____	____

Evaluation Codes: OQ=oral questions; TT=teacher-made test; CT=commercially-made test; TO=teacher observation.

MATHEMATICS

ANNUAL GOAL: Brian will improve his mathematics achievement to a grade score of 5.0 on the WIAT achievement test by June, 1995.

INSTRUCTIONAL OBJECTIVE:	TYPE EVALUATION:	DATE COMPLETED:
1. Brian will be able to estimate a given line segment alongside a rule in inches with at least 90% accuracy.	____	____
2. Brian will be able to solve a word problem requiring knowledge of the value of coins (penny, dime) with at least 90% accuracy.	____	____
3. Brian will be able to solve a one-step addition problem (when read to him) with at least 90% accuracy.	____	____
4. Brian will be able to solve a one-step subtraction problem involving money with at least 90% accuracy.	____	____
5. Brian will commit his addition and subtraction facts to memory and be able to reproduce them in spoken or written form with 100% accuracy.	____	____
6. Brian will be able to add a row of three one-digit numbers presented horizontally with 100% accuracy.	____	____
7. Brian will be able to subtract two two-digit numbers that require no renaming with 100% accuracy.	____	____

Evaluation Codes: OQ=oral questions; TT=teacher-made test; CT=commercially-made test; TO=teacher observation.

ACCEPTANCE OF AND AGREEMENT TO IMPLEMENT IEP

I accept this IEP as the educational plan that will meet the needs of my child. Furthermore, as my child's home teacher, I agree to abide by the requirements and stipulations of this IEP during the course of the present school year and will implement it by planning and delivering individualized instruction based on the instructional objectives specified herein.

_____
David or Jennifer Davis
Home School Teacher

_____
John P. Doe
Special Education Consultant

_____
Date

Note: No consultant signature would be necessary if parents were writing the IEP on their own. The parent's signature alone would designate a self-contract.

5

Program Practices

Planning daily schedules, evaluating student work, and recording grades are examples of educational procedures that teachers should be able to perform skillfully and automatically. These procedures add the structure and organization that is necessary to make school days run smoothly. A more important benefit is that students know what to expect from their teachers and how to perform successfully when these educational procedures are practiced consistently. This chapter discusses the procedures we believe are needful and appropriate for parents who teach struggling learners at home.

Basic Materials and Equipment

Home schools are characterized by their individualization and flexibility. In fact, little is required for a parent to set up shop, save a location and a child. Even the educational materials used by home educators vary from one family to another. But for parents of struggling learners, we have found that certain basic materials and equipment are essential if instruction is to flow smoothly.

Figure 5.1 provides a list of basic teaching materials and equipment that are essential, particularly when the home program includes *remediation* and *regular* instruction components. While it is understandable that many parents may not have the immediate funds to purchase all of these materials right away, they probably should begin purchasing items from this list on a regular basis until all have been purchased. Although this is certainly not an exhaustive list, many of these materials correspond with one or more of the teaching techniques discussed in Chapters 6, 7, 8 and 9:

Figure 5.1

Basic Equipment and Materials

- Index cards (all sizes)
- Colored markers (bright colors)
- Manipulatives (popsickle sticks, marbles, jacks, buttons, etc.)
- Highlighter pens
- Pencil grips
- Electronic spell checker
- Computer (with color monitor and printer)
- Color construction paper
- Graph paper (¼-inch scale)
- Audiotape player-recorder
- Headphones
- Blank cassettes
- Solar calculator
- Small white board (with markers)
- Portable study carrel

Classroom Arrangement

The location of the home school classroom and the arrangement of furniture and equipment are two important considerations in teaching struggling learners. As for location of the classroom, our experience has been that parents need to be aware of a couple of things. One is that many, if not most, struggling learners have attention and distractibility difficulties. And two, these children will need more monitoring than other children in the household who may not have learning difficulties; hence, the classroom will need to be within close proximity of the parent.

We believe that, when feasible, the home classroom should be a separate room that has been set aside in the home for the sole purpose of education. At the same time, though, we recognize that the typical family will not own a mansion that has multiple floors of rooms just waiting to be occupied (really!). It may be that another existing room in the house will also have to serve as the home class-room (e.g., dining room). For many mothers who find that they have to shuffle teaching responsibilities with other household duties, the dining room, in fact, may be the central-most location in the home and more easily accessible for most of the school day. It is our experience that two rooms in particular, the child's bedroom and the family room, can be very distracting and too comfortable for struggling learners. Parents should probably steer clear of using either one of these rooms for the primary instructional setting.

With regard to arranging furniture and equipment, we recommend the floor plan in Figure 5.2, if you have a separate room in the home that can be designated solely for instruction. This floor plan allows for a separate storage closet, in addition to file cabinets, where more frequently used instructional materials can be stored and retrieved quickly. It also provides a central work place (i.e., the work table) where parents can work directly with their struggling learner on regular and remediation activities. The study carrel, where the student can concentrate on independent tasks, needs to be in a stimulus-free corner of the classroom and completely away from the busier parts of the classroom where typically there is more traffic.

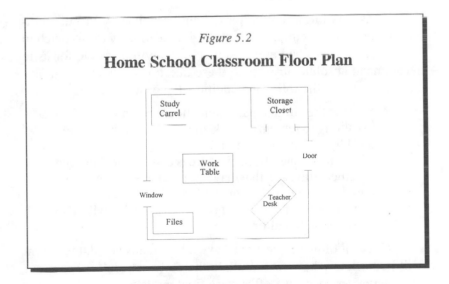

Figure 5.2

Home School Classroom Floor Plan

Daily Schedule

Home instruction for struggling learners should include a consistent daily schedule of activities. In developing a daily schedule that meets their unique needs, parents should consider the following questions:

- How much total time will be devoted to instruction each day?
- How much of the total daily instructional time will be allocated to remedial instruction?
- How much of the total daily instructional time will be allocated to regular instruction?
- How much time will be allocated to each individual subject?
- How much of an individual subject will be devoted to direct skill teaching versus independent seat work?
- Which subjects need to be taught first or earlier in the day?
- How much time should be allocated to transition between lessons?
- How will remedial and regular lessons be ordered throughout the day?

Answers to these questions should revolve around the individual needs of the child. Since struggling learners vary so much in their specific needs and abilities, it is virtually impossible for us to recommend absolute answers to these questions. Parents will also need to consider the following additional questions:

- What is the child's maximum attention span, based on his ability to remain on-task and engaged in instruction once he comes to attention?
- What are the specific subject areas that are most in need of remediation and that may deserve more instructional minutes each day than others?
- Are there other children in your home who will also need instructional time?

Once all of these questions have all been answered, the parent will better know how to formulate the daily schedule. From our teaching experiences, we offer these final guidelines:

- For elementary age youngsters, always begin the morning with a brief discussion of such things as the day's date, the day of the week, the season of the year, temperature, and an overview of the day's activities. This helps struggling learners, particularly students with disabilities, be more aware of their immediate life and surroundings.
- Add in movement-type activities (e.g., activities in other rooms, physical activities, etc.) throughout your daily schedule so that students will not be tempted to become sleepy or lazy.
- Alternate academic lessons with non-academic subject lessons. For example, parents might open the day with a Bible or language arts lesson. The next period of instruction may be music, art, physical education, etc. This provides a contrast in learning for the student.
- Students with more severe limitations in learning, attention, or behavior will need to have more daily instructional time allocated for remediation, which means that there will be less time for regular instruction.

The schedule should be written out showing the time each subject lesson is to begin, break times, recess, lunch, outings, and so on. It should be posted in a prominent place in the home classroom and followed as closely as possible (Let your answering machine monitor your phone calls so you can stick to your schedule!) Remember, the degree to which the parent follows the daily schedule will affect in the long-run the amount and quality of structure that is provided to the student. Above all, parents must remember that they are always a model of behavior, either acceptable or unacceptable, before their children. Children will naturally imitate their parents. It logically follows, then, if parents consistently follow the daily schedule, they should expect their children to reciprocate. In Figure 5.3, we provide a sample daily schedule of a learning disabled boy who has two areas of academic remediation.

Figure 5.3

Daily Schedule for an LD Student with Two Areas of Remediation

Time	Subject	Materials & Equipment	Assessment
8:30 to 8:40	Overview of day		
8:40 to 8:55	Bible	Textbook; workbook	Workbook–90%
8:55 to 9:15	Reading (remedial)	Fernald; DI; Cloze	Oral questions–100%
9:15 to 9:35	Reading (regular)	Textbook; workbook	Workbook–90%
9:35 to 9:50	Physical exercise		
9:50 to 10:00	Reading (remedial)	Review; firm-up	Oral questions–100%
10:00 to 10:20	Math (remedial)	Strategy training; CAI	CAI items–90%
10:20 to 10:35	Math (regular)	Textbook; workbook	Workbook–90%
10:35 to 10:50	Fine arts activity		
10:50 to 11:00	Math (remedial)	Review; firm-up	Written items–90%
11:00 to 11:15	Writing (regular)	Textbook; workbook	Workbook–90%
11:15 to 11:30	Spelling (regular)	List; 5-step strategy	Oral quiz–100%
11:30 to 11:45	Recreation		
11:45 to 12:00	Science/History	Textbook; workbook	Workbook–90%

Evaluating School Work

One of the most important organizational procedures is evaluating (i.e., *grading* or *scoring*) a child's educational performance. Not only will children realize their success (or lack thereof) from proper evaluation of school work, but parents will benefit by knowing whether or not they are making progress in meeting the needs of their children.

Record a grade everyday. Evaluating a struggling learner's school work properly begins by determining that you will record a grade everyday for each of the child's subject areas. Consistent, daily evaluation and recording of the child's progress is one of the only ways that a parent can know whether the child is really learning. Evaluation may mean giving tests eventually, but it doesn't mean that you have to give a formal, written test everyday. To the contrary, if a parent has just introduced a new skill (e.g., in reading, spelling, math, etc.) on a given day, she certainly wouldn't give a full-blown written test the same day (although some would argue that this serves as a form of pretesting). Parents need to find informal ways of evaluating their child's degree of success everyday.

Use responses to oral questions. You can informally measure a child's success by keeping a mental count of the number of correct answers he gives from oral questions that you ask during the lesson. Of course, we are making an assumption that you will be asking a number of oral questions as you directly teach skills to your child (see Chapter 6 on questioning as an effective teacher behavior). For example, suppose a teacher asks approximately ten oral questions during a literature lesson, and the child misses only two. The child's *success rate* for that day's lesson, therefore, would be 80% (i.e., he answered 8 out of 10 questions correctly).

Use independent seat assignments. Keeping a record of correct response rates to oral questions is only one way of measuring a child's academic performance. As you continue teaching (and re-teaching) a skill on successive school days, you may decide to give the child some independent assignments such as worksheets, brief projects, and so on (eventually full-blown tests) to determine how well he is mastering the skill.

It is important that the score for seat assignments reflect *independent* performance on the part of the child with no help or assistance from the parent. While a lesson may at some point include written tasks where the parent provides close monitoring and immediate corrective feedback (e.g., helping the child do a math problem), all lessons should conclude with a separate seat assignment that the child must complete on his own. It could be as brief as five math problems or five comprehension questions on a reading passage.

Record percentage or raw scores. Parents should consistently record the child's success rate each day. Regardless of the type of assignment (i.e., oral questions, worksheet, test, project, etc.) you are scoring, the success rate would mathematically be the number of correct answers divided by the total number of questions to which the child responded. The score would then be recorded as a percentage. However, some parents may feel more comfortable recording the *raw score* or the number correct. For example, a parent could record "5/7" in her gradebook for a child who gets 5 out of 7 correct math problems.

We recognize that this is a highly quantifiable system of measuring child progress. For struggling learners whose progress may not be as obvious or as pronounced from one day or one week to the next, we suggest that parents mathematically assess the child's mastery of skills on a daily basis so that both they and the child will be able to realize steady and consistent progress as it occurs. Quantifying successful learning tasks in children can be difficult sometimes, but it will be much easier if parents make sure that skills and learning tasks they teach can be *observed* (i.e., the parent must see, hear, or both see and hear the skill being performed).

Determining Mastery

How will parents know when their child has mastered a skill or concept? Mastery has been attained when a child demonstrates that he can consistently perform a skill at a designated proficiency level (or success rate) over a sustained period of time. Determining mastery, then, requires that parents answer two questions: (1) What level of proficiency will I expect of my child? and (2) How long must he perform the skill at that level?

Proficiency levels for skills will vary, depending on the severity of the child's disability and the type of skill involved, be it academic, social, or behavioral. For students with moderate to severe retardation, for example, proficiency in a skill may only mean being able to perform the skill successfully with 75% to 90% accuracy. Yet for others with mild forms of disability (e.g., learning disability or attention deficit disorder), the expected proficiency could be higher, say 90% to 100% accuracy. Generally, parents should require higher percentage rates for basic skills such as reading functional sight words or calculating arithmetic problems using the basic operations. Yet when more advanced reading, writing, and math skills are being taught, the predetermined proficiency level might be somewhat lower.

As to how long shall a child demonstrate the expected proficiency level, we believe that a child has attained mastery of a skill when he can sustain the predetermined success rate (e.g., 90% success) for at least *three* consecutive school days. Children with milder forms of disability will reach their mastery rates sooner than children with more severe disabilities. Whatever the case, parents must exercise patience and faithfully continue teaching, reteaching, encouraging, and reinforcing the skill until the child can show the percentage goal for at least three school days running.

In order to prevent regression in learning, parents will need to review mastered skills periodically as other new skills are introduced. Flynn contends that home teachers will "want to aim for improvement, not necessarily mastery [for]....Mastery can discourage you because it takes...special children so long to get there."[1] Parents who have children with more severe learning, attention, or behavior difficulties may need to consider Flynn's advice when children are not able to show mastery, even with repeated presentations and trials of the skill.

Recording Progress

Careful record-keeping is important in many areas of our lives. Parents must not underestimate the importance of proper record-keeping in documenting the progress of their children.[2] The Home School Legal Defense Association strongly urges parents to "keep accurate records that explain how you met [the child's] needs and how your child has progressed."[3] With the volatility of the disability rights movement in America and the ever-increasing attention of government to the education of disabled students, we believe that careful record-keeping is especially important for home educators who have children with bona fide disabilities. We recommend that, for each of the child's academic subject areas, the home teacher's gradebook include a daily record of the following:

- date of lesson;
- IEP objective addressed;
- specific skill taught;
- form of evaluation; and
- student's success rate for that day.

A simple spiral notebook or ring-binder will suffice for the gradebook. Figure 5.4 shows one entry in a sample gradebook. In this example, the lesson for the day addressed a math skill, counting by tens, which was an objective required on the child's IEP. The mother used oral questions (OQ) as the form of evaluation. After she taught the lesson, which included careful modeling of how to count by ten, she gave her child five attempts to count orally by ten up to one hundred on his own. He was able to do so accurately four out of five attempts for an 80% success rate. Devising codes for identifying the IEP objectives (e.g., "Math #3" means the third math objective on the child's IEP) and the form of evaluation (e.g., "OQ" means oral teacher questions) simplifies recording.

Figure 5.4

Gradebook Record for a Math Lesson

Date	IEP Objective	Skill/Lesson	Measure	Percentage
2-18-95	Math #3	Counting/10s	OQ	80%

Graphing Progress

A gradebook benefits the teacher mostly, since it is an organizational tool. The written record of IEP objectives and mastery rates contained in gradebooks have little meaning or relevance for students. Yet struggling learners need to be ever aware of where they stand in their school work. Bar graphs and line graphs are excellent ways to pictorially present a child's mastery rates (either percentages or raw scores) so that he can understand how well he is improving. Graphs work well with both academic and behavioral skills. Consider the two examples in Figure 5.5.

Developing a Permanent Folder

Conventional educators, particularly special educators, take pride in how carefully they document a student's progress through the school years. But then again, they must, because federal and state education laws require that schools maintain proper records on a child during his school enrollment. For most public and private schools, a permanent folder is initiated when a child enters the school system, and the folder follows the child as he moves from one grade to the next. The permanent folder will contain many documents that describe the child's physical, intellectual, academic, and behavioral

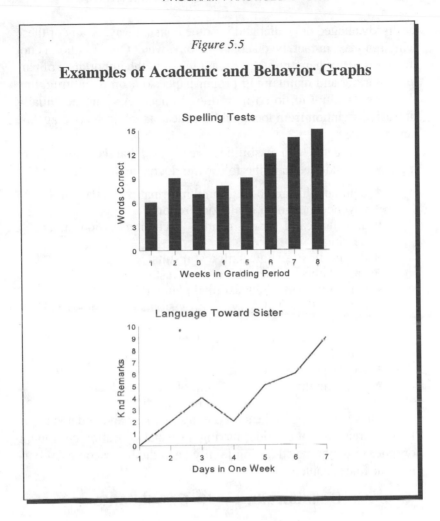

Figure 5.5

Examples of Academic and Behavior Graphs

development and progress. We believe that home educators should also keep permanent folders. It is especially important to do so, if a child has a disability (see Chapter 1).

We have mentioned previously that the field of special education finds its roots in the volatile civil rights movement in the 1960's and 1970's. Even today, one doesn't have to look far to find inordinate media attention directed toward children with unique needs. Pick up a newspaper on almost any given day or channel surf on the television only briefly and you will find a bleeding heart for a child who is disadvantaged or challenged in some unusual way. Many of these children may, in fact, be disabled in some way. Our intention is not to be insensitive here; rather, we want to stress the importance of parents starting and maintaining proper paperwork on their struggling learners. Failure to do so may draw unnecessary and potentially intrusive attention from local public educators, child service agents, and the like.

For students with disabilities, we suggest that the home school permanent folder contain the following documents:

- demographic and background information on the child
- psychoeducational evaluation reports
- annual health exam results, including vision and hearing
- diagnostic academic skill test results
- annual one-on-one achievement test results
- annual individual educational plan (IEP)
- record of related service provisions (e.g., physical therapy)
- record of contacts with and recommendations from consultants
- copies of all report cards
- representative samples of school work products

These items should be stored in a safe place and updated regularly. Parents might consider having a special education consultant or other close, home educating family keep duplicate copies of permanent folder contents.

Collaborating with Consultants

Seeking the advice and counsel of others who may have more wisdom and experience is a practice clearly taught in Scripture (Proverbs 12:15). One way to get extra help and assistance in teaching struggling learners at home is by collaborating with an educational consultant.[4] By definition, a consultant is one who "gives professional or technical advice."[5] Clearly, based on what we have discussed to this point, teaching struggling learners requires skills that go beyond what is needed to teach typical learners. The field of special education can be a highly technical one, and parents who educate a child with a disability at home may need professional advice and assistance from time to time, perhaps more frequently when they first begin.

Although the technical assistance aspect in and of itself is sufficient justification for consultants, there is one additional, perhaps more compelling reason for parents to consider collaborating with a special education consultant—legal support. HSLDA provides the following admonition:

> Because of the legal complexities involved in dealing with schools and government agencies, one of the safest things you can do to protect your home school is to obtain the services of a special needs educational consultant. This consultant would be someone who could, in the event HSLDA was called upon to defend your home school, serve as an objective expert witness...[6]

If parents are collaborating with a consultant on a regular basis, the consultant should be able provide the necessary documentation and testimony to corroborate the quality of parents' teaching efforts, if litigation ensues. Grace Flynn, a home educating mother of a son who has Down Syndrome, believes that obtaining assistance from a special education consultant, "is for our benefit, so that we do a good job and are not found wanting in the event of a court case."[7]

A qualified special education consultant "can be anyone who has either credentials or experience in the same area as [the] child's special need."[8] We believe that the best candidates for special education consultants are those who hold professional credentials (i.e., a college degree and/or license) and experience in the field of special education. For the most part, parents should be able to find a well-prepared and well-credentialed special education consultant from one of the following groups:

- public or private school special education teachers;
- retired special education teachers;
- learning specialists who operate private clinics; and
- professors of special education at the university level.

We recommend that parents first check with local home school support groups or state home school associations who may keep a list of available special education consultants. Home School Legal Defense Association also maintains a current list of special education consultants from different regions of the country. The National Challenged Homeschoolers Associated Network NATHHAN (see Appendix A) in Washington state may be able to assist parents in securing special education consultants. Finally, if all else fails, parents might consider making contact with one or more of the private schools in their community to see if they have special education teachers who could be employed in the after-school hours as consultants.

Scott Somerville,[9] special needs attorney with HSLDA, recommends that parents make contact with their consultant periodically throughout the school year. In general, when it comes to instructional matters, the more parents make contact with the consultant, the more efficient the home education program may be. HSLDA's[10] general recommendation is that parents and their consultant make contact a minimum of four times during the school year.

The number of contacts will also vary according to the experience of the parent and the severity of the child's disability. For parents who are novices at teaching children with disabilities at home or whose child may have a severe-profound disability (e.g., severe mental disability), we recommend that parents make monthly contact with the consultant during the course of the first school year. For the second school year, we recommend that the number of contacts fade to every other school month (e.g., September, November, January, etc.). For the third and succeeding school years, four contacts with the consultant should be sufficient, provided the child's progress is at a level that is satisfactory to the parent.

Consultants typically charge a fee for their professional services. But we believe that, when parents get to the point that they need outside help, the invested money will be well worth it in the long-run. Parrish, a home educating mother of a health impaired son, testifies that, "Consulting special education teachers...[have] helped [me], and the importance of this guidance cannot be stressed enough..."[11]

---

[1]Flynn (1994), p. 43
[2]Lapish (1994)
[3]HSLDA (no date), p. 1
[4]Lapish (1994)
[5]*American Heritage Dictionary* (1985)
[6]HSLDA (no date), p. 2
[7]Flynn (1994), p. 43

[8]HSLDA (no date), p. 2
[9]Somerville (1994)
[10]HSLDA (no date)
[11]Parrish (1995), p. 44

6

Modifying Instruction

Most struggling learners will have to be taught differently if optimal learning is to occur. Traditional teaching approaches are generally not effective with them. While simple presentations using standard textbooks and workbooks or giving extra time and practice may be sufficient for average learners, they likely will not work with struggling learners. These students need modifications in instruction and perhaps intensive teaching methods in order to succeed at rates that correspond with their God-given abilities.

The remainder of this chapter will focus on how parents can adapt and modify instruction. We begin with a discussion of how teacher behaviors can be altered. We conclude with ideas on how parents can provide modifications and accommodations in instructional materials and the learning environment for learners who struggle.

Modifying Teacher Behavior

Altering one's teacher behavior may seem a bit peculiar to some parents. After all, when we speak of changing behavior per se, we typically have students in mind, not teachers. But researchers have identified a number of teacher behaviors that, when implemented deliberately and systematically by the teacher, will make significant differences in how children learn.

For example, Nowacek, McKinney, and Hallahan[1] compared teacher behaviors of regular classroom teachers and special education teachers. They discovered that special educators showed *more* of the following teacher behaviors when teaching students with disabilities than did regular teachers in traditional classrooms with nondisabled learners (the asterisk "*" indicates significantly more):

- **Monitoring***—the teacher provides careful oversight and supervision of learning experiences for the child, while giving regular assistance and structuring of the child's responses to questions.
- **Questioning**—the teacher asks questions on information taught in the lesson and questions about the student's work.
- **Praise***—the teacher delivers specific positive, verbal statements for acceptable performance that are reinforcing to the child and gives a reason for praise, rather than giving general, global praise.
- **Positive Regard***—the teacher motivates the child by urging him to work harder, provides him with reassurance that he is moving in the right direction, and recognizes that his unique needs may require various instructional modifications.

Nowacek and her colleagues also discovered that special education teachers showed *approximately the same* amounts of the following teacher behaviors as did regular classroom teachers:

- **States Expectations**—the teacher provides an introduction to the lesson by reviewing with the student, states exactly what will be studied during the lesson, and states precisely what the student will be required to do after the lesson concludes.
- **Makes Assignments**—the teacher brings the lesson to an end by reviewing and summarizing what was taught, checks to make sure that the student understands what was taught, brings likely mistakes to the child's attention, and clearly states instructions for assignment and what she expects of the student.

Finally, Nowacek and her associates found that special education teachers showed *less* of the following teacher behaviors than did regular classroom teachers (the asterisk "*" indicates significantly less):

- **Negative Regard***—the teacher ignores the needs of students and shows little tolerance for their characteristic behaviors.
- **Effective Transitions**—the teacher prepares the student for changes in the lesson when different activities will be occurring.

In another teacher effectiveness study, Sutton, McKinney, and Hallahan[2] investigated some of the same teacher behaviors as the prior researchers, but with special education teachers who taught mildly disabled students versus special education teachers who taught severely disabled students. Highlights of their findings follow (the asterisk "*" indicates significantly more or less):

- Teachers of severely disabled students **give more negative regard*** than did teachers of mildly disabled students.
- Teachers of severely disabled students **acknowledge misbehavior more*** than did teachers of mildly disabled students.
- Teachers of severely disabled students **desist, rebuke, warn, threaten, and punish more*** inattentive and disruptive behavior in severely disabled students than did teachers of mildly disabled students.
- Teachers of severely disabled students **ignore more** inattentive and disruptive behavior than did teachers of mildly disabled students.
- Teachers of mildly disabled students **state expectations more** than did teachers of severely disabled students.
- Teachers of mildly disabled students **give more positive regard** than did teachers of severely disabled students.
- Teachers of mildly disabled students **make assignments more** than did teachers of severely disabled students.

- Teachers of mildly disabled students **give answers more** to student-initiated questions/comments than did teachers of severely disabled students.

Only a handful of other studies to date[3,4,5,6,7,8,9] have examined effective teacher behaviors of teachers of students with mild disabilities such as mild mental retardation, learning disabilities, and emotional-behavior disorders. A consensus of their statistical findings reveals that teachers of struggling learners will do *significantly more* of each of the following:

- **Ask more questions** during a lesson;
- **Allow more trials** in answering questions correctly;
- **Elicit more correct responses** to questions;
- **Tell fewer answers** so students can figure it out on their own;
- **Give more positive feedback** and **more negative feedback**;
- **Provide more support** and **more encouragement**;
- **Deliver shorter lessons**;
- **Include more concept examples** in lessons (for illustration);
- **Provide greater lesson structure** (e.g., objectives, introductions, explanations, summaries, and reviews); and
- **Provide more monitoring of assignments**.

We believe that home teachers who implement these teacher behaviors in their daily instruction will maximize learning success in their children. Concentrating on one or two teacher behaviors per week, rather than trying to implement all of these at once, may be the most effective way of incorporating these into your daily instruction.

Modifying Instructional Processes

Fouse and Brians contend that, "For many ADD students, all that is needed to help [them] succeed in school are some modifications in assignments and tests."[10] We agree and suggest that modifying and accommodating for instruction is critical to the success of *all* struggling learners, not just ADD students. Some struggling learners may eventually need the additional benefit of instruction presented through more intensive teaching techniques (see Chapters 7, 8, and 9). Generally, modifications are given to a student in order to help him compensate for or work around a barrier or limitation in his life that may be preventing him from learning at optimal levels using regular educational procedures.

Regardless of the type or degree of modification, one principle should be kept in mind. Instructional modifications and accommodations are legitimate and appropriate only if academic integrity is preserved and not compromised in the learning process. That is, when modifications give the student an edge or advantage over average learners rather than allowing him to compensate for and work around the barrier of his limitation, then the modification ceases from being of any real educational value to the child. For example, it would be difficult, if not impossible, to justify allowing an ADD student to use a calculator to complete a mathematics assignment, when he has no prior history of learning difficulties in mathematics. Giving him a calculator would in effect reduce the quality of his learning by preventing him from exercising his computational skills.

One of the most comprehensive collections of instructional modifications that we have identified to date is Cohen's[11] *Instructional Modification Menu* (See Figure 6.1). Home teachers will find these ideas immensely practical and helpful. In addition, a number of other instructional modifications and accommodations have been discussed by researchers in several recent studies.[12,13] Many of these ideas are directly applicable to parents who have struggling learners. Consider these accommodations for students in the areas of test-taking, giving directions for assignments, and using a tape recorder.

Test-taking

Parents may need to alter one or more of the following variables with children who struggle as they take tests in the home school:

- Test administration
- Number of test items
- Student response mode

Test Administration. Tests are traditionally administered to students in written form. But teachers make a number of assumptions when giving written tests to students. Some assume that children have adequate visual processing and reading decoding skills, to mention a few. But struggling learners typically have limitations in these areas. Therefore, it is not only appropriate, but necessary that

Figure 6.1

Instructional Modification Menu

1. Use a study carrel
2. Set-up room dividers
3. Have student wear headsets to muffle noise
4. Seat child away from doors or windows
5. Seat child near model (parent teacher, peer, or sibling)
6. Vary working surface (e.g., floor or vertical surface)
7. Simplify, shorten, or amplify directions
8. Give both oral and written directions
9. Have student repeat directions
10. Have student repeat lesson objective
11. Change cognitive or difficulty level of question
12. Change response format (e.g., written to spoken)
13. Provide sequential directions
14. Use manipulatives or concrete materials
15. Alter expected objective criterion or proficiency level
16. Reduce number of items on assignments or tests
17. Highlight relevant or key words, phrases, and features
18. Use rebus (i.e., picture) directions
19. Provide more practice trials
20. Increase allocated time
21. Develop and teach a step-by-step strategy for the task
22. Change type of reinforcer (e.g., edible, tangible, activity, etc.)
23. Increase amount of reinforcer given at one time
24. Increase number of times child receives reinforcer
25. Delay reinforcement
26. Increase response wait-time after a question
27. Use specific rather than general praise
28. Have peer or sibling serve as tutor or checker
29. Provide frequent review
30. Have student summarize at end of lesson
31. Use self-correcting materials
32. Adapt test items for differing response modes
33. Provide mnemonic devices
34. Provide tangible reinforcers
35. Establish routines for handing in work, etc.
36. Use timers to show allocated time
37. Provide visual cues (e.g., posters, banners, etc.)
38. Block out extraneous stimuli on written material
39. Tape record directions
40. Tape record student responses
41. Use a study guide
42. Provide critical vocabulary list for content material

43. Provide basic math fact list during math assignments
44. Use clock faces to show classroom routine times
45. Use dotted lines to line-up math problems or show margins
46. Provide transition directions between adjacent activities
47. Assign only one task at a time
48. Provide discussion questions before reading assignments
49. Use word markers to guide reading lines of text in books
50. Alter sequence of presentation
51. Enlarge or highlight key words on test items
52. Provide a daily or weekly assignment sheets
53. Post a daily or weekly schedule
54. Use graph paper for place value or during computation of digits
55. Establish rules and review frequently
56. Teach key direction words (e.g., circle, underline, define, etc.)
57. Allow student to use a pencil grip
58. Tape assignment paper to desktop surface
59. Shorten project assignments in daily tasks
60. Break directions down into segments
61. Number or order assignments to be completed
62. Place student's desk closer to black board
63. Incorporate wholesome, currently popular themes and characters into lessons
64. Repeat major points in a lesson before concluding
65. Use verbal cues while speaking (e.g., "One...two....," "Don't write this...")
66. Pause appropriately after emphasis points during lesson presentations
67. Change tone of voice (e.g., loud to whisper) and inflection (e.g., high to low)
68. Collect notebooks periodically to check accuracy of notetaking
69. Reorganize tests so that items progress from easy to hard
70. Color code place value tasks
71. Use self-teaching materials
72. Do only odd or even numbered items on long assignments or worksheets
73. Use a typewriter or computer word processor
74. Provide organizers (e.g., cartons, bins) for desk materials
75. Teach student scanning and skimming skills for varied reading rates
76. Provide written summaries of content taught during lesson
77. Use peer-mediated teaching strategies (e.g., buddy system)
78. Call student's name before asking a question
79. Use extra line spaces between lines of text
80. Color code materials or directions
81. Provide calculators for higher order math problems
82. Circle math computation sign
83. Use hand signals to cue behavior (e.g., attention, responding)

Adapted from *Instructional Modified Menu* (pp. 201-203) by S. Cohen (1993), *Effective Instruction: Principles and Strategies for Programs*, in B. S. Billingsley (Ed.), *Program Leadership for Serving Students with Disabilities*, Richmond, VA: Virginia Department of Education. Reprinted by permission.

tests be modified to meet their needs. For example, home teachers may need to read the test items orally to the child or possibly even administer the test on computer rather than on paper for a multisensory effect and to increase the child's motivation.

The parent could also dictate the test items on a tape recorder, and the child could pause, rewind, and replay as needed. The more direct application of audiotaped tests may be in history, geography, and science where understanding and mastery of content is the goal, not demonstration of decoding skills per se. For example, if the child has a learning disability in reading, then giving him a science test in written format may not allow him to show what he has learned. He probably won't get past the barrier of having to read the questions on the test. In order to compensate for time required to press and release tape player keys, parents should allow students extra time to complete audiotaped tests.

Number of Test Items. The number of test items can also be modified. For example, a child is scheduled for a unit test on adding three-digit numbers with and without regrouping. A typical test may include 10 problems on addition with no regrouping and 10 problems on addition with regrouping for a total of 20 problems. For LD students with processing difficulties, however, 20 problems may be too many to complete at one setting. An appropriate accommodation would be to reduce the number of problems to maybe 5 to 7 of each of the two types of addition problems for a total of 10 to 14 problems. Although there are fewer total items on the test, the teacher still gets an adequate sampling of the child's mastery.

Student Response Mode. Finally, you can alter how the student responds to test questions. Many educators in conventional and home schools alike place too much emphasis on written responses. It may surprise some parents to know that nothing is etched in stone, theoretically speaking, when it comes to students providing written responses to test questions. Conventional educators typically require written test responses many times to facilitate large groups of students in their classrooms. Recognizing, however, that struggling learners may have certain limitations that prevent them from responding in written form (e.g., an LD in written expression), parents may have to obtain their answers to test questions in different ways. If we allow these students to speak their answers, dictate them on audiotape, or key them into a computer, we are allowing them to work around their writing barrier and still be able to show what they have learned.

We must be ever aware of our primary goal in giving tests. For example, the goal of science and history tests is to assess a student's mastery of content-specific skills, not to determine whether he is adept at the underlying processes or prerequisite skills in test-taking such as reading decoding and handwriting. Making the modifications recommended earlier for test-taking should preserve the academic integrity for which we are striving, yet allow the struggling learner to show that he has mastered the expected material. We believe it is important that parents make written notation on the test as to the specific modifications that were allowed the student for documentation purposes.

Giving Directions for Assignments

Giving directions for assignments is an integral part of any teacher's daily routine. Although teachers of average learners many times resort to an almost conversational, non-deliberate style when delivering directions, parents of struggling learners will often find this tyle ineffective. Not only are struggling learners' listening and attention skills noticeably weaker, they also process information with greater difficulty. Parents, therefore, will need to employ a more intentional, deliberate means of giving directions to these students before they approach learning tasks.

The Council for Exceptional Children recommends the following ideas to teachers who work with ADD students. We believe these suggestions are applicable to any struggling learner.

- Use more than one modality [e.g., show it, say it, etc.] when giving directions.
- Use alert cues [e.g., say, "Eyes right here..."] to get attention before giving directions.[14]

Garnett offers these additional recommendations, which are directed to teachers of ADD students. Again, we believe these ideas can be used just as successfully with any struggling learner:

- Ensure a good amount of eye contact when giving verbal instructions.

- Make directions clear and concise. Simplify, when needed.
- Be consistent with daily instructions.
- Be sure the youngster comprehends *before* beginning the task. Have him/her repeat instructions in *words* [aloud back to the teacher].
- If you need to repeat, do so with the understanding that it is legitimately needed. Remember, being clear, kind and firm is a model for how the youngster will treat *himself* and others.
- Help the youngster learn to seek help appropriately (many children...will not ask).
- Provide the structure of a daily assignment book, monitoring the accuracy of what gets written in it [i.e., the actual assignment pages, number of problems, etc.]...[15]

As with modifying your teacher behaviors, you may wish to concentrate on incorporating just one of these ideas per week rather than tackling them all at once. Gradually integrating these ideas on giving directions one at a time will allow you ample time to perfect one before adding in another. It also allows the student the necessary time he needs to adjust to slight changes in your instruction rather than bombarding him with all of them at once. Parents of struggling learners who implement these ideas gradually and enforce them consistently will see a noticeable change in the academic performance of their child in the long-run.

Modifying With A Tape Recorder

Integrating a simple piece of technology—the audiotape recorder—into the instructional blueprint for struggling learners in the home school should increase the likelihood that they will succeed.[16] What follows are ideas on how home teachers can modify instruction using audiotape recorders in reading, writing, and spelling tasks.

Reading Tasks. Struggling learners typically have difficulties in reading decoding and comprehension. Try audiotaping textbook chapters for them to use in reading tasks where content, not reading skills per se, is the goal of the assignment (e.g., a history or science lesson). Audiotaping textbooks can be a laborious project, but securing help from friends and volunteers like older siblings in the household, grandparents, home educating neighbors, or church members can greatly reduce the parent's burden. C. Mercer and A. Mercer[17] offer these guidelines in preparing audiotapes:

- Tape in a fully-furnished room to absorb noises.
- Turn the volume low before recording to avoid clicks on the tape.
- Fade the volume before stopping.
- Vary readers to reduce boredom.
- Identify chapter titles and page numbers at the beginning.
- Ring a bell to signal the end of a page.
- Pause at paragraph divisions to allow for reflection and absorption.
- Record a brief beginning message instructing the student to listen properly, to stop and take notes occasionally, and to turn the page at the bell.

Students should always use headphones and follow the printed text visually as they receive auditory support from the tapes. This encourages active learning and allows for greater content absorption.

Parents may want to consider securing ready-made audiotaped textbooks from Recordings for the Blind (RFB). This organization will provide audiotapes for any textbook upon request. If RFB does not have tapes for a certain book, you need only notify them in advance, and they will prepare the tapes at no charge. RFB does require a nominal one-time fee (around $75), and a special tape player must be purchased or leased in order to use the tapes (See Appendix A for mailing address).

Writing Tasks. Use the tape recorder as a medium for students who have difficulties getting thoughts from their heads to paper. Have the student develop a rough outline (2 to 3 major points with 2 to 3 subpoints) on the topic he will be writing about. Using the major points and subpoints, the student will then dictate his thoughts (in complete sentences) on the tape recorder. The student should avoid dictating his entire paper in one sitting. Encourage him to focus on one major point at a time. Once the entire paper has been recorded on tape, the home teacher can then assist in transcribing the dictated material via typewriter or computer word processing as well as helping the student with error monitoring for corrections before turning the paper in to be graded.

Spelling Tasks. Struggling learners can also be taught how to use the tape recorder for studying and testing in spelling. The student should first record his spelling words on tape, leaving a 5-second pause between each word. The student can then administer practice tests to himself at home. Using headphones will help block out interfering noises. The student should be instructed to use the pause and stop buttons to allow more time for processing and writing out the words. The parent should allow the student to self-administer final spelling tests for the week using dictated spelling word tapes he has prepared.

Once more, we recommend that parents keep a record of the types of instructional modifications and accommodations they allow their children. For example, it would be wise to note on the first page of a science test that the student was allowed to speak his answers, or that the test items were dictated to him, and so on. As we will address in greater detail in Chapter 11, this is part of the necessary documentation that parents of struggling learners must be careful to keep on their child.

Modifying Learning Environment

While adapting teacher behavior and various instructional processes are important, parents of struggling learners must be careful not to downplay the potential effect that the learning environment can have on a child's ability to "produce, achieve, create, problem-solve, or learn."[18] As we noted in Chapter 3, the learning environment can be assessed formally via commercially-produced learning style inventories or tests. These tests can be administered by parents in the home under the supervision of a qualified diagnostician. Test results would include recommendations on how to modify the child's learning environment. Figure 6.2 provides the results of a learning style inventory administered to a 14-year old homeschooled ADD student.

Parents can informally assess a child's classroom setting by manipulating particular learning style variables on their own and noting changes in the child's school performance. For example, noise level can affect a child's learning. Try allowing the child to complete his reading or math assignment in a completely quiet room for three to five consecutive schools days. Then allow him to complete his assignment with soft instrumental music playing in the background

Figure 6.2

Learning Preferences of an ADD Student

Preference	Learning Variable	Preference
Quiet	**Noise Level**	*Sound*
Dim	Light	*Bright*
Cool	Temperature	*Warm*
Informal	**Room Design**	*Formal*
Low	**Motivation**	*High*
Low	**Persistence**	*High*
Low	**Responsible**	*High*
Less	Lesson Structure	*More*
Alone	Learns with Others	*With Peers*
No	**Authority Present**	*Yes*
No	Learns Several Ways	*Yes*
No	Auditory Learning	*Yes*
No	**Visual Learning**	*Yes*
No	**Tactile Learning**	*Yes*
No	**Kinesthetic Learning**	*Yes*
No	**Food Intake**	*Yes*
Evening	Learning Time of Day	*Morning*
No	Late Morning Learning	*Yes*
No	Afternoon Learning	*Yes*
No	**Mobility During Lesson**	*Yes*
Low	**Parent Motivated**	*High*
Low	**Teacher Motivated**	*High*

Note: The student indicated no strong preference for non-bold faced learning variables.

for another three to five school days, and compare the results to see if there are differences. Struggling learners may not have clear preferences for all types of learning style variables, but our experience has been that they will show clear inclinations for some. Once these preferences are identified, parents should modify the learning environment accordingly in order to maximize the child's school success.

---

[1]Nowacek, McKinney, & Hallahan (1990)
[2]J. Sutton, McKinney, & Hallahan (1992)
[3]Englert (1983)
[4]Englert (1984)
[5]Englert & Thomas (1982)
[6]Haynes & Jenkins (1986)
[7]Kaufman, Agard, & Semmel (1985)
[8]Leinhardt, Zigmond, & Cooley (1981)
[9]Sindelar, Smith, Harriman, Hale, & Wilson (1986)
[10]Fouse & Brians (1993), p. 29
[11]Cohen (1993)
[12]Nelson & Lingnugaris-Kraft (1989)
[13]Bursuck, Rose, Cowen, & Yahaya (1989)
[14]Council for Exceptional Children (1994), p. 11
[15]Garnett (1991), p. 4
[16]J. Sutton & C. Sutton (1994)
[17]C. Mercer & A. Mercer (1989)
[18]Price, R. Dunn, & K. Dunn (1985)

7

Generic Teaching Methods

M ost parents are familiar with traditional teaching approaches like discussion, drill and recitation, lecture, projects, teaching games, independent study, and so on. While average learners generally succeed with these methods, struggling learners do not. When instructional modifications and accommodations (see Chapter 6) are combined with traditional approaches, however, some struggling learners will survive quite nicely. For others, though, particularly those with bona fide disabilities, parents may need to employ one or more intensive teaching methods during times of regular or remedial instruction to maximize success.

From our experience and reading of the literature, we have identified a number of special teaching methods that can be easily implemented by parents. What is remarkable about these methods is that they can be used in teaching just about any subject, including reading, mathematics, history, and science.

Direct Instruction

Direct instruction has been characterized as *active teaching*.[1] Good describes the active teacher as one who provides brief presentations and demonstrations of information and concepts. The teacher also provides feedback to student recitations and questions as well as follow-up assignments that include instructions and practice examples. Monitoring of student progress is important in active teaching, and the teacher gives additional feedback and reteaches when necessary.

Direct instruction is a teaching method that can be used successfully in teaching virtually any subject area where the student is required to master academic performance skills in reading, mathematics, science, and social studies. Commercially-produced direct instruction programs are available, for example, *Reading Mastery*: *DISTAR Reading*[2] and *DISTAR Arithmetic I, II, and III*.[3,4,5] Parents may find that the generic direct instruction procedure discussed by Becker, Engelmann, and Thomas[6] more than sufficiently serves their purpose in teaching the struggling learner at home without having to make the tremendous investment in purchasing the commercially packaged programs.

The direct instruction model by Becker and associates[7] includes nine carefully ordered steps. In using direct instruction to teach individual skills to the student, the teacher must provide a(n):

1. **Attention Signal**—The teacher calls the student to attention by using a language or verbal cue such as, "Johnny...eyes on me!" or "David...listen to me!"
2. **Task Stimulus**—The teacher presents (models) the task through verbal explanation, a textbook example, picture cards, white board, easel, poster, or other visual/auditory/tactile/kinesthetic stimulus (e.g., a list of spelling or reading words on a poster).
3. **Stimulus-Direction**—The teacher instructs the student to attend to the stimulus by saying words like "Look here..." or "Listen, please."
4. **Stimulus-Prompt**—The teacher helps the student attend to one or more specific characteristics about the stimulus by describing, expanding, or illustrating.
5. **Response-Prompt**—The teacher zeros in on exactly what she expects the student to know; here the teacher explicitly says or shows the student what he will have to say or show in the question to follow.

6. **Response-Direction**—The teacher questions the student about the skill or task that was taught and includes in her question how the student will respond (e.g., say, write, point, etc.).
7. **Do-It Signal**—The teacher cues the student to respond by using a perceptual cue, for example, a hand drop, tap on desk, finger snap, or language-verbal cue (e.g., "Write you answer now.").
8. **Task Response**—The student gives the answer to the teacher's question or does what she asks by speaking, writing, or doing some action, depending on what was indicated by the teacher in Response-Direction.
9. **Reinforcer**—The teacher rewards the student for his correct response (e.g., apple slices, stickers, tokens) and combines it with a social reinforcer (e.g., "Good job on those spelling words!")

One complete cycle of this procedure will take no more than a minute or two. Parents may use direct instruction numerous times in a single lesson as they apply it to teaching different steps or subskills that comprise a larger task or skill. Sometimes one cycle may need to be repeated several times in succession using different examples or illustrations. Following the order of the steps in direct instruction is critically important, so parents may need to practice and rehearse the procedure several times prior to the actual lesson until it becomes automatic. Figure 7.1 provides an example of a parent using direct instruction in teaching a telling time concept.

Cloze Technique

Conventional educators have used the Cloze[8] technique primarily as an informal assessment tool with students who have reading comprehension difficulties.[9] Luftig describes how this technique works:

This technique involves selecting passages of approximately 260-275 words of varying degrees of difficulty. Words are then deleted from the passages and the child is asked to write in the missing words. In order to write in these missing words, the child needs to glean contextual clues from the surrounding words and sentences in the

Figure 7.1

Direct Instruction with Telling Time Skill

Attention Signal:	"Jared...(tap on desk)...Look this way!"
Task Stimulus:	(Mother shows picture of clock face with 12 marks)
Stimulus-Direction:	"Look...(pointing)...at this clock."
Stimulus-Prompt:	"See...it has 12 marks. You remember last week we learned that each hour of the day has 60 minutes."
Response-Prompt:	"Well...each mark here represents 5 minutes out of a 60-minute hour."
Response-Direction:	"On a scrap piece of paper, write the number of minutes that each mark stands for on this clock."
Do-It Signal:	"Do it now."
Task Response:	(Jared writes the number "5" on scrap paper.)
Reinforcer:	"Terrific!" (Mother gives Jared an apple slice .)

passage. The logic is that the ability to glean such contextual meaning from surrounding phrases is a sign of reading comprehension.[10]

Levey[11] suggests that the Cloze technique can also be adapted for use in developing reading comprehension skills in children. She recommends that teachers follow these steps in constructing reading comprehension activities for students who add or omit words during reading or for students who are whole-word readers:

1. Choose a passage of 100 words at the child's functioning reading level.
2. Leave the first and last sentences in tact, but for all sentences inbetween, leave every fifth or tenth word blank.
3. Provide the list of missing words that correspond in correct order with the blanks in the reading passage.
4. Have the student read the passage and place the words from the list on the blanks.

5. Once mastery has been achieved with this format, construct additional passages, but provide a list of missing words in mixed order from which the student may choose.

6. Succeeding word lists should include only selected words [not all missing words] in mixed order, which forces the student to use contextual clues to determine the remaining missing words;

We believe the Cloze technique can be further adapted for use in teaching math skills. Consider the example of solving linear equations in Figure 7.2.

Figure 7.2

Cloze Technique Applied to Solving a Linear Equation

Equation Steps					Fill-In List	
$5x$	$- 9$	$= 2x$	$+ 3$			
$-2x$		$- \square$			$2x$	
$\square - 9$		$= 0x$	$+ \square$		$3x$	3
$3x + \square$	$=$	$+ 9$			9	
$3x$	$=$	$\square$			12	
$3x$	$=$	12				
$\square$		3			3	
x	$=$	$\square$			4	

Solution: $x = 4$

Strategy Training

Responsible, independent adults use step-by-step strategies on a regular basis to solve many of their routine, day-to-day tasks and problems. For example, a mother goes through several steps mentally in preparing for grocery shopping:

1. Are the children coming ?
2. Do I have my shopping list?
3. Do I have the checkbook or cash?
4. Do I have coupons?
5. Will I take the car or truck?
6. Do I have to be back home at a certain time?

Our recommendation that strategy training be used as a special method to teach struggling learners should be no surprise to parents. Strategies are simply a normal part of life. Many parents and teachers make the assumption that children already have sufficient learning strategies to accomplish learning tasks. Although some average learners do demonstrate good strategies and know when to use them, students with disabilities generally do not. Parents, therefore, need to teach strategies directly and intentionally to struggling learners in order for them to be strategy efficient.

Deshler defines *learning strategies* as "techniques, principles, or rules that enable a student to learn, solve problems, and complete tasks independently."[12] There are many different types of learning strategies that children will need to be taught including organization, study, review, memory, assignment completion, time management, and test-taking strategies. Learning strategies "can be used in all content areas, as well as for developing appropriate social skills."[13] More important, learning strategies help students learn *how* to learn.

We are aware of one student whose task was to master the basic elements of the U. S. Constitution. In order to organize the material so that it could be learned and remembered more efficiently, the student formed various mnemonics and acrostics. For example, one of the questions in his study guide was "By what means has the Constitution been changed since its adoption?" The answer was "amendments, court decisions, and presidential practices." The student devised the mnemonic CAP "C" for court decisions, "A" for amendments, and "P" for presidential practices.

In like manner, parents can design strategies for their children at any time and for just about any learning task. But strategies don't always have to be in the form of an acrostic. They can be as simple as breaking a learning task down into its sequential steps, listing them on an index card or paper, and having the child check off the steps of the strategy as he completes them. Note in Figure 7.3 a checklist strategy for writing research papers that we developed for a young man a couple of years ago.

Fouse and Brians describe the process of developing and teaching a strategy as follows:

> In strategy instruction the teacher first determines the curriculum [or task] demands with which the student is having difficulty and then matches a learning strategy to meet the specific demands. In teaching the strategy, the instructor determines the student's current learning habits and then describes and models the new learning strategy. The student should verbally rehearse the strategy and practice with controlled materials [i.e., hand-selected by the teacher and done under the teacher's observation and supervision] followed by classroom materials. The teacher then evaluates to determine student mastery of the strategy.[14]

A critical step in teaching a strategy is to talk with the student and make sure that he understands the inefficiency of his previous way of approaching and solving a learning task. Getting a student to this point may require a series of one-on-one conferences or discussions. The parent may even need to review with the student, preferably in private, some samples of his tests, papers, worksheets that illustrate inefficiencies. Until the student recognizes that his former way of accomplishing a task is indeed inefficient then he will probably not be willing to accept a new learning strategy. As with teaching almost any new skill to a child (e.g., rollerskating, bike riding), parents need to exercise patience with themselves and with the child in this phase of strategy training.

Also, parents must not underestimate the importance of modeling the strategy for the student before expecting him to perform it independently. Modeling, of course, is greatly emphasized in Scripture, both directly and indirectly. The Lord Jesus Himself came to

Figure 7.3

Research Paper Strategy

<u>Directions</u>: Complete the steps in the order presented. Before you begin, determine due dates for each of the steps and record these dates in the blanks provided. As you finish individual steps, record your completion date.

<u>Due Date</u>	<u>Completed</u>	<u>Tasks</u>
_____	_____	1. Research your topic and locate 5 or 6 journal articles (make xerox copies of the articles).
_____	_____	2. Have someone audiotape any articles that you have difficulty reading.
_____	_____	3. Read or listen to each article at least two times without using a highlighter or writing anything down.
_____	_____	4. Read each journal article a third time, and use a highlighter pen to mark passages in the articles that support the topic you've chosen.
_____	_____	5. Make bibliography notecards on each of the articles you intend on citing in your paper. Make sure you record the following information about each article:

    (1) authors;
    (2) title of article;
    (3) date of publication;
    (4) title of journal;
    (5) volume and issue numbers; and
    (6) beginning and ending page numbers.

| _____ | _____ | 6. Make notecards on passages that you highlighted in your journal articles. Prepare notecards using the following strategy: |

    (1) Reread the highlighted passage in the article.
    (2) Ask yourself what are the most important things to write down.
    (3) Close your eyes, and write these thoughts in your own words.
    (4) Record any key sentences or phrases that you intend on using as quotes (use " ").

Due Date	Completed	Tasks
_____	_____	7. Develop and write your thesis statement.
_____	_____	8. Develop and write 3 major points for your paper (points A, B, and C on your outline).
_____	_____	9. Develop and write 3 supporting thoughts for each of your major points (these will represent subpoints 1,2, and 3 for each of your major points A, B, and C on your outline.).
_____	_____	10. Take each of your major points A, B, and C on your outline and match them with corresponding thoughts on your journal notecards.
_____	_____	11. Using your notecards, go to a quiet place and develop a main sentence and several supporting sentences that will comprise one paragraph that corresponds with point A, subpoint #1. Use a tape recorder, and dictate your thoughts speaking in complete sentences. Do this procedure for each of your remaining points and subpoints. Do only one paragraph per day.
_____	_____	12. When all paragraphs for each major point and subpoint have been dictated and recorded on tape. Have a typist transcribe your sentences and paragraphs exactly as you have dictated them. Ask the typist to use a word processor, run the spell-check and grammar-check programs, and make appropriate corrections before saving the file to disk.
_____	_____	13. Print out a draft of your paper. Use the COPS error-monitoring strategy and make any corrections that the computer may have missed. Have your typist make corrections on the computer.
_____	_____	14. Follow format guidelines specified by your teacher before printing out your final copy.

this world not only to provide a way of salvation for sinful man but to model a godly life for us. The written Word of God presents numerous models of men and women who loved God and served Him with all their might. Biblical models were provided so that we might imitate and incorporate in our lives the same principles of character and Christlikeness. So it is when modeling is applied to strategy instruction. Parents must sufficiently model the strategy for the child prior to holding the child responsible for using the strategy in learning tasks.

Musical Mnemonics

Children, like adults, get much enjoyment from music. Music can also be relaxing. Dunlap[15] recommends that parents listen to Baroque-style music in order to deal with the extra pain and stress that is brought on at times when home educating struggling learners. But music is more than just a means of relaxation or source of aesthetic pleasure. In short, it can be used to help people accomplish their work. It is not unusual to hear someone humming or whistling a tune as they are working. Many businesses will play music for their customers or clients (e.g., department stores, grocery stores, physician's office, etc.) while they shop or receive a service. Some employers use music to maximize the work performance of their employees (e.g., assembly lines). In an educational sense, we know that music can be used to assist students in learning and remembering subject matter information.

The ability of a child to recall and remember information accurately is one indicator that effective learning has occurred. That's what a *mnemonic* is designed to accomplish. Use of mnemonics in teaching is not a novel idea, however. I can still remember in my early grade school years sitting next to my grandmother on the piano bench for lessons. Like many other piano teachers, she employed mnemonics to teach the various key positions in the bass and treble clefs. For example, the word, "FACE" helped me to remember the order of the notes in the spaces on the treble clef.

Gfeller reviewed available studies that investigated the effectiveness of *musical mnemonics* with mentally retarded or slow children and concluded that the "heightened attention and the optimal balance of redundancy and novelty in musical stimuli contribute to improved recall of information."[16] From a practical perspective, we know this is true. Very few of us who came from functional homes with caring, loving parents escaped learning the traditional ABC jingle. In our work with disabled students, we always found it interesting that even those with very low ability (i.e., IQ's in the retardation range) could recite the ABC song with just as much fluency as children with normal to above normal ability.

Gfeller suggests that musical mnemonics can be used when teaching learning tasks that reflect factual information (e.g., math facts, states and capitals), procedural steps and rules (e.g., grammar rules), and motor activities when self-monitoring is needed (e.g., constructing letters during writing). Gfeller further adds that it is important to choose a familiar tune, if possible, on which to construct the mnemonic and that, once developed, it should be "demonstrated, practiced, and finally reinforced"[17] with the child.

Parents may wish to follow these steps in developing and teaching musical mnemonics:

1. Select a tune.
2. Apply the lyrics [i.e., the steps of the desired skill].
3. Model the musical mnemonic several times for the child.
4. Have the student sing along with you [reinforce promptly].
5. Have the student sing the mnemonic alone [reinforce promptly].
6. Have the student gradually fade from singing overtly, to humming, to using an inner voice [reinforce promptly].
7. Monitor the child's application of the mnemonic [reinforce promptly].

Figure 7.4 provides an example of a musical mnemonic. Developed by Haffner and Ireland,[18] this mnemomic teaches about nouns and is set to the tune of "Old MacDonald had a Farm."

Commercially-produced musical mnemonics programs are available. For example, Audio Memory[19] in California produces song kits that cover a variety of academic skills such as grammar (parts of speech, punctuation rules, Greek and Latin roots, writing exercises, etc.), geography (names and locations of continents, oceans, planets and 225 countries), states and capitals, and multiplication, addition,

Figure 7.4

Musical Mnemonic for Teaching Nouns*

I spy nouns, oh yes I do.
N-O-U-N-S.
Names of people, places, and
things—
N-O-U-N-S.
With a common noun here,
And a proper noun there.
Here's a name, there's a name,
Everywhere are more names.
I spy nouns, oh yes I do.

*Sung to the tune of *Old MacDonald Had A Farm.*

and subtraction facts. The kits contain echo-style audiocassette song tapes, teacher's guides, posters, and illustrated songbooks and workbooks.

Another company, *Sing 'n Learn*[20] also produces audiocassette song tapes that cover the following topics that may be of interest to parents of struggling learners: (1) Ballads of American History; (2) Sing, Spell, Read and Write; (3) Math and Science; (4) Grammar and Handwriting; (5) History and Geography; (6) Foreign Languages; (7) Scirpture Memory; (8) Music Education and Art; and (9) Bible, Historical and Character Building Stories. Appendix A provides the addressses and toll-free numbers for both *Audio Memory* and *Sing 'n Learn*.

Computer-Assisted Instruction

Computerized gadgets and toys dazzle most children. It seems that, when nothing else will capture a child's attention, a computer can. We are convinced that parents who work with struggling learners should capitalize on the computer's capability to motivate children to learn. Computers provide a number of instructional benefits for children with learning difficulties:

- A multisensory approach to learning;
- A wide range of learning rates;
- Immediate feedback;
- The capability to record, store, and recall student responses; and
- Varied forms of positive reinforcement.

There are literally thousands of educational computer software programs on the market today. Therefore, choosing the right ones that are most effective from an instructional perspective can be difficult. Unfortunately, some computer programs can be considerably expensive. If parents don't choose wisely, they can unintentionally sink an entire school year's allocated money for instructional materials in useless software.

Although there are some educational software programs in the public domain realm that are useful with struggling learners, our experience has been that much of what is available is simply not sensitive to the unique needs of struggling learners. One quarterly publication, *Special Times*,[21] reviews hundreds of software titles from a wide variety of vendors to determine the ones most appropriate for children with learning disabilities. The *Special Times* review board believes that choosing software with the following eight characteristics will ultimately be most effective for struggling learners:

- Provides substantive (hopefully corrective) feedback to the student;
- Has an appropriate reading level that will not present a barrier to the student in absorbing and mastering the content of the program;
- Allows choices (e.g., picking content, different strategies, etc.);
- Does not require absolute correctness on answers to questions, but allows the student several opportunities to get the correct answer;
- Does not limit the student on the amount of time or the number of times to respond to questions;
- Allows the student to choose difficulty level;
- Has an attractive screen that is uncluttered and does not distract the student from focusing on the learning task; and

• Has directions that are brief and optional and do not cause the student to have to rely heavily on the teacher for assistance.

Parents can secure a free subscription to the *Special Times* magazine by contacting Cambridge Development Laboratory via letter or toll-free number (see Appendix A). The magazine categorizes reviewed software in three areas: (1) language arts; (2) mathematics; and (3) essentials (i.e., gradebook programs, IEP programs, speech synthesizer programs, etc.). Prices begin around $29.95.

[1]Good (1979)
[2]Engelmann & Brunner (1988)
[3]Engelmann & Carnine (1972)
[4]Engelmann & Carnine (1975)
[5]Englemann & Carnine (1976)
[6]Becker, Engelmann & Thomas (1975)
[7]Becker, Engelmann & Thomas (1975)
[8]Taylor (1953)
[9]Luftig (1987)
[10]Luftig (1987), p. 177
[11]Levey (1984)
[12]cited in C. Mercer & A. Mercer (1989), p. 494
[13]Fouse & Brians (1993), p. 32
[14]Fouse & Brians (1993), p. 32
[15]Dunlap (1994)
[16]Gfeller (1986), p. 28
[17]Gfeller (1986), p. 29
[18]Haffner & Ireland (1990)
[19]Audio Memory (1996)
[20]Sing'n Learn (1996)
[21]Cambridge Development Laboratory (1995, Spring)

Chapter

8

Teaching the 3 R's

W hile the methods discussed in Chapter 7 would be useful in teaching just about any subject, other intensive techniques are more appropriate when teaching the 3 R's—Reading, 'Riting (i.e., writing), and 'Rithmetic (i.e., arithmetic). In this chapter, we discuss key teaching methods that have been used by special educators in teaching children with disabilities. Parents will find these techniques both user friendly and easy to implement in the home for struggling learners.

Reading Techniques

Probably the most prevalent area of learning difficulty among school-age children today is reading. Most parents recognize the critical importance of reading and the havoc it can reek on the lives of students who are poor readers. Not only is reading important for reading sake, but minimal reading skills are necessary if children are to absorb content in other subjects including science, history, and so on. More important still, the ability to read is an absolute requirement for a person to reach some semblance of success and independence in adult life.

Multisensory-VAKT Method

Professional educators tell us that 80% to 90% of classroom instruction is visual in nature. Therefore, students who are strong visual learners would stand to profit the most. But for struggling learners who may learn better through auditory, kinesthetic (movement), or tactile (touch) means, the strong visual emphasis of traditional instruction places them at a disadvantage.

The multisensory approach allows learners to input information from instruction using all four input channels concurrently (i.e., visual, auditory, kinesthetic, and tactile; hence, the acronym VAKT). Fichter explains that "With more senses actively involved in the learning process, there is...greater likelihood that the student will receive and process more information about the subject being taught"[1] through multisensory instruction.

Dr. Grace Fernald,[2,3] one of the great special educators this century, is credited primarily with pioneering the multisensory approach. She used it as a remedial method with students who had serious learning problems, particularly in reading. Some special educators have successfully applied the VAKT approach to teaching spelling, vocabulary words, and arithmetic facts. In the area of reading, the multisensory approach can be used in teaching whole-word reading (e.g., teach "horse" as a whole word, not by its phonetic parts, "h-or-se"). A great advantage to this approach is that it allows poor readers the opportunity to build a basic reading vocabulary quickly. While this is good, we believe that a balanced approach[4] to teaching reading to struggling learners will also include some phonics instruction.

Fernald's VAKT Technique. The complete procedure for teaching a single word or math fact using the multisensory-VAKT method should take no more than two to five minutes. The parent will need the following materials:

- 3 x 11 inch strips of paper (typing paper cut three times length-wise would work nicely);
- bold-colored markers or crayons that appeal to the child;
- 3 x 5 or 4 x 6 inch lined, index cards;
- index card box;
- lined notebook paper;
- pencils and pens; and
- computer and printer or typewriter.

The Fernald multisensory approach, as described by C. Mercer and A. Mercer,[5] contains four stages through which the student gradually progresses. The student should remain at the lower stage until he can show a high degree of mastery of words or math facts over a consistent period of time. A synopsis of the stages follow:

Stage 1. The teacher writes the word or math fact on a paper strip. The student looks (visual) at the word or fact, while tracing (kinesthetic) the letters or numbers with his finger (touch) and listening to himself (auditory) pronounce or read it. The child repeats this process (perhaps up to a half dozen times) until he is ready to write the word or math fact on separate paper without looking at the strip. If he makes an error, he must go through the multisensory procedure for several more repetitions, and then attempt to write it again without error. Once the word or math fact is learned, the student records the word on an index card and files it alphabetically in the box (math facts are filed according to fact families, e.g., adding with 2's, multiplying by 5's, etc.). The student is then instructed to write a brief sentence or story using the word (or write a word problem using the math fact). The story (or word problem) is subsequently typed so that the student can see and read the word (or math fact) in print.

Stage 2. The teacher writes the word or math fact on a paper strip. In this stage, however, the student only looks (visual) at the word or math fact on the paper strip and pronounces or reads it (auditory) repetitively until he believes he has it mastered (no tracing). He then writes it on separate paper correctly without error and files it accordingly in the card box. The student continues to write stories (or word problems).

Stage 3. The paper strips are removed at this stage, and the student learns the word or math fact directly from a piece of paper, as it is written (in manuscript or cursive). The student does no tracing or oral pronunciation or reading and is not required to write the word or math fact in this stage. The student may begin reading books at this stage, and the teacher reviews continually words or math facts (filed previously).

Stage 4. The student needs no isolated printing of the word or math fact on separate paper and can "recognize new words by their similarity to printed words or parts of words already learned and thus can apply reading skills and expand reading interests."[6]

The multisensory approach remains very popular among special educators today and continues to be a widely used teaching approach in many remediation programs. However, Kavale and Forness[7] caution that its effectiveness is inconclusive at this time. They indicate that some studies show that the multisensory approach produces positive results for some children, but it makes no significant difference with others.

Neurological Impress Method

The *neurological impress method* or NIM[8] is a remedial reading technique that may prove to be attractive to home educators who are on a shoe-string budget, since the only instructional material required to implement this method is a reading book. C. Mercer and A. Mercer describe NIM as a technique that involves "joint oral reading at a rapid pace by the student and the teacher...based on the theory that a student can learn by hearing his own voice and someone else's voice jointly reading the same material."[9] Using a reading book (as is, with no special preparation or alterations) that is on a level slightly below the student's present reading level, the parent can implement the NIM technique as follows:

> The student is seated slightly in front of the teacher, and the teacher's voice is directed into the student's ear at a close range....The objective is simply to cover as many pages as possible in the allocated time, without tiring the student. At first, the teacher should read slightly louder and faster than the student, and the student should be encouraged to maintain the pace and not worry about mistakes. The teacher's finger slides to the location of the words as they are being read. As the student becomes capable of leading the oral reading, the teacher can speak more softly and read slightly slower, and the student's finger can point to the reading. Thus, the student and teacher alternate between leading and following.[10]

Parents should make sure that the learning environment is free from the noise and distractions of other children when using the NIM technique. Clearly, the NIM technique will give the struggling learner more experiences in reading decoding and oral reading rate than in comprehension per se. It may be wise, then, to combine oral questions and discussion activities with the NIM technique in order to foster comprehension and understanding of the material.

Computer-Assisted Reading

As we discussed in Chapter 7, integrating computers in daily instruction should yield great benefits for struggling learners in all subject areas. Reading is no exception. From our review of the reading computer software programs cited in the *Special Times*[11] magazine, we recommend the titles listed in Figure 8.1. We caution Christian parents to screen these programs carefully, as some may have objectionable, non-Christian elements (e.g., wizardry, the underworld, etc.).

Figure 8.1

Reading Computer Software

Title	Grades	Vender	Computers
Phonics Pinball	K-4	SWEPS Educ.	AP
Stickybear Reading	K-5	Optimum Resource	AP/IBM
Reader Rabbit 1,2,3	K-6	The Learning Co.	AP/IBM/MAC
Word Magic	2-6	Clearvue/SVE	AP
Reading Rodeo	K-4	Heartsoft	AP/IBM/MAC
Reading Fun	1-6	Troll Software	AP
Syllable Squares	3-12	Junior Software	AP
Treasure Drive: Reading...	3-12	Gamco	AP/IBM
Vocabulary Machine	1-12	Southwest/EdPsych.	AP/IBM
Word Launch	1-12	Teacher Support	AP/IBM/MAC
Word Attack Plus!	4-12	Davidson	AP/IBM/MAC
Developing Reading Power	4-7	Clearvue/SVE	AP
Word Munchers	1-5	MECC	AP/IBM/MAC
Back to the Story	1-8	Focus Media	AP
Stickybear/Comprehension	3-6	Optimum Resource	AP/IBM
Reading Comprehension	3-8	Heartsoft	AP/IBM/MAC

Note: AP=Apple; MAC=Macintosh.

Spelling Techniques

Learning to spell proficiently presents major headaches for most students with disabilities and for countless other struggling learners (not to mention their parents!). Little wonder this is the case, for spelling requires a child to possess adequate abilities in a number of cognitive skills including visual imagery, visual memory, auditory discrimination, and so on. Unfortunately, many children with disabilities have weakness in one or more of these cognitive skills.

Gordon, Vaughn, and Schumm[12] reviewed 17 research studies that investigated the effectiveness of various spelling interventions used by professional educators who taught LD students. They identified a number of teaching techniques that produced statistically significant increases in LD students' spelling performance. We discuss these in the paragraphs that follow.

Error Imitation and Modeling

The parent should first reproduce in written form the student's misspelled rendition of the word, then model the correct spelling of the word, preferably on the line directly beneath the misspelled word. We suggest using 1/4-inch graph paper (one letter per square), which will allow for vertical alignment of the letters between the misspelled and correctly spelled words. In a one-to-one correspondence manner, the child should be able to see his errors more readily. Parents can emphasize the student's errors even more by using a colored pen to highlight vertically the corresponding pairs of missed and correct letters. Parents should continue to provide repeated presentations of error imitation followed by modeling of single words until they are confident that the child fully understands. Like other intensive teaching methods that we have illustrated in this book, error imitation and modeling is time-consuming. But Fulk and Stormont-Spurgin add that, "peer tutors [or older siblings] can be trained to employ these simple procedures."[13]

Learning Fewer Words Per Day

Elementary spelling textbooks generally present 18 to 25 spelling words per lesson. The typical learner is expected to master one spelling lesson each week. It is not unusual for conventional elementary teachers to pre-test the student on the entire spelling list for a given lesson early in the school week. The students then study and practice the whole set of spelling words until the final test is given near the end of the school week. Although many typical learners may already know the majority of the spelling words at pre-test time and will, hence, have only a few words to master for the remainder of the week, it is just the opposite with struggling learners. They may perform poorly at pre-test time and be overwhelmed the remainder of the week with having to master virtually all of the words.

Our experience has been that a more incremental approach is necessary if children with learning difficulties are to succeed in spelling. That is, only a few words from the list should be directly taught and practiced each day until the entire list has been mastered. From their research on effective spelling interventions, Gordon and her colleagues found that "overload and interference in spelling instruction"[14] may be avoided if teachers present no more than *three* spelling words per day to the student. If parents abide by this recommendation and combine it with continuous review from one day to the next, then the child should be able to accumulate around 15 mastered spelling words per week.

Practicing Through Movement

Goldstein maintains that, "What we do repeatedly we [will eventually] do automatically."[15] We see this principle illustrated in organized athletics. Basketball coaches are notorious for making their players practice set plays over and over again prior to a game, so that the plays will be executed in a fluid, efficient manner during game time. This concept of repetitive practice is also applicable to learning academic skills, including spelling.

Although some conventional teachers may argue to the contrary, researchers have concluded that having the child practice spelling words repetitively through movement activities such as copying the word numerous times on paper, tracing templates or letter tiles, and even typing the word repeatedly on a conventional typewriter or computer keyboard increases spelling performance. In choosing a particular repetitive practice activity, it is important for teachers to "consider students' preferences [which are] likely to increase motivation to practice and learn."[16]

Spelling Strategies

We have already discussed the importance of strategy training (see Chapter 7) with struggling learners. Using strategies in teaching spelling represents just one subject-area application. It is clear that, when students have an organized, systematic approach to learning spelling words, rather than just capriciously looking at the words as a way of trying to learn them, they tend to be more successful. We believe that one of the best strategies to use is Stage 1 of Fernald's multisensory approach (illustrated in Chapter 7). Parents should make sure that students follow the steps in order when they attempt to learn spelling words.

Self-questioning Strategy. Wong believes that effective spelling instruction "appears to [require] two components: knowledge of phonics...and knowledge of spelling strategies."[17] She developed a spelling strategy, which she tested in a study that involved eight sixth-grade students who qualified for remedial spelling instruction. Prior to teaching the spelling strategy, however, teachers in the study provided the following spelling instruction to each of the students:

- Pronunciation and meaning of words
- How to break words into syllables
- The structure of the words
- Decomposition of words into root word plus suffix (or prefix)
- Explanation of suffix (or prefix) concepts
- How words changed with the addition of suffix (or prefix)

The teacher then taught the students the following self-questioning spelling strategy (a series of questions the students were instructed to ask themselves during the spelling test):

1. Do I know this word?
2. How many syllables do I hear in this word? [Write down the number.]
3. I'll spell out the word.
4. Do I have the right number of syllables down?
5. If yes, is there any part of the word I'm not sure of the spelling? I'll underline that part and try spelling the word again.

6. Now, does it look right to me? If it does, I'll leave it alone. If it still doesn't look right, I'll underline the part I'm not sure of the spelling and try again. [If the word I spelled does not have the right number of syllables, let me hear the word in my head again, and find the missing syllable. Then I'll go back to steps 5 and 6.]

7. When I finish spelling, I'll tell myself I'm a good worker. I've tried hard at spelling.[18]

Wong reported that, prior to the teaching of the spelling strategy, the students could only demonstrate about a 30% spelling accuracy rate. Two weeks later, after the students had used the spelling strategy and were expected to demonstrate 100% mastery of a set of spelling words, a follow-up post-test showed that these students were still able to spell the words at almost an 80% accuracy level. Based on these results, it appears that teaching a struggling learner to use this self-questioning spelling strategy may increase his spelling performance. Parents should have little trouble adapting this strategy for use in the home.

5-step Strategy. Graham and Freeman[19] developed a spelling strategy that is similar to Stage I of Fernald's multisensory-VAKT method (see Chapter 7). The strategy includes vocalizing and tracing components. Students will need 3 x 11 inch paper strips, colored markers, line paper, and pencils in order to apply the strategy. The student will repeat the 5-step strategy as many times as necessary to master individual spelling words. The steps to the strategy are as follows:

1. Say the word.
2. Write and say the word [on line paper].
3. Check the word [for correct spelling].
4. Trace and say the word [on paper strip].
5. Write the word from memory and check spelling.

Computer-Assisted Spelling

We discussed earlier in Chapter 7 some of the advantages and benefits of using computers as part of the instructional program for struggling learners. Gordon and her colleagues conclude from available research that "computer lessons can enhance spelling performance and increase motivation to learn by capitalizing on students' interest."[20] From our review of the spelling computer software programs reviewed in *Special Times*[21] magazine, we recommend the titles listed in Figure 8.2. Again, Christian parents are urged to check these programs carefully for objectionable elements.

Figure 8.2

Spelling Computer Software

Title	Grades	Vender	Computers
Crosswords	3-12	Mindplay	AP/IBM/MAC
Lucky Seven Spelling...	3-12	Intellectual Soft.	AP/IBM
Spell It! Plus	5-12	Davidson	AP/IBM/MAC
Spelling Mastery	2-4	DLM/SRA	AP
Spelling Puzzles & Tests	K-12	MECC	AP
Spelling Rules	3-12	Optimum Resource	AP

Note: AP=Apple; MAC=Macintosh.

Mathematics Techniques

When compared to the other academic subjects, particularly reading, educators and researchers have paid less attention[22] to developing and discovering remediation techniques and methods in mathematics that work best with struggling learners. Nonetheless, we have identified a number of methods that we believe are effective with children who struggle and that can be easily implemented by parents in the home.

Concrete-Pictorial-Symbolic Approach

Many educators, including C. Mercer & A. Mercer,[23] recommend the use of concrete objects or manipulatives in the early stages of teaching basic math skills. Mastering mathematics through tactile (touching) and kinesthetic (movement) activities as part of a child's early learning experiences is a concept that is firmly grounded in Piaget's theory of cognitive development. Once a child shows mastery of a skill via *concrete* learning, then the teacher may gently lead him into *pictorial* learning experiences. The final stage of organizing and mastering knowledge would be at the *symbolic* level. The concrete-pictorial-symbolic teaching method, typically referred to as the *cognitive-developmental approach*, is one of the most important that parents can implement for struggling learners.

We believe that students who continue to show delays in basic math skills may never have been sufficiently exposed to concrete or pictorial learning experiences in their early years. It is unfortunate that many math textbooks begin instruction at the symbolic level. Occasionally they will provide lessons with a pictorial learning emphasis, but rarely do you see math instruction commencing at the concrete or manipulative level of learning. We urge parents to put careful thought into how the teaching of math skills can be developed through a series of methodical lessons that progress from the concrete, to pictorial, and finally to the symbolic levels of learning. This method of teaching will be especially critical when teaching older students who have struggled for years without demonstrating mastery of basic math skills. We illustrate this approach by showing how parents might teach place value.

Concrete Level. The parent should secure several empty soup cans and, as a school activity, have the child decorate the cans using construction paper. The child should label each of four cans with the words, *Ones, Tens, Hundreds,* and *Thousands.* Each decorated can should be a different color (e.g., *Ones*=red; *Tens*=blue; *Hundreds*=green; *Thousands*=Orange) to help the student distinguish them better. Several dozen popsicle sticks are also needed.

The parent can then teach several lessons, demonstrating to the student how to group the sticks in bunches of tens, hundreds, etc. Continue grouping activities until the student can show mastery. The student is then taught how to place a representative stick in corresponding cans for groups of ten, one hundred, etc. Continue lessons of this sort until mastery occurs. When the child can take a given set of popsickle sticks and place representative sticks in the appropriate corresponding place value cans with 100% success, then mastery has occurred. Some struggling learners may need to spend several days to a week or more in this concrete phase of learning before moving on to the pictorial level of learning.

Pictorial Level. In this level of learning, the parent develops a series of worksheet activities (easy to do these days with computer graphics programs!) that would include pictorial representations of colored place value soup cans and popsickle sticks that the student used in the concrete level of learning. On these worksheet activities, the student would be expected to do with paper-and-pencil what he did in the concrete learning activities. For example, one worksheet might include five different sets (quantities) of colored popsicle sticks (probably colored tally marks) along the left side of the worksheet, and a corresponding picture set of the four colored and labeled soup cans along the right side of the worksheet.

The student would then be instructed to circle groups of ten tally marks, one hundred tally marks, etc. and place a representative tally mark for each of the ten or one hundred groups in the corresponding pictured soup cans. For example, if there were 34 tally sticks in one set, then the student would circle three groups of ten, and leave four single tally marks. He would then place one representative tally mark for each of the ten-groups, for a total of three, in the corresponding pictured *Tens* soup can, and four representative tally marks in the *Ones* soup can. Again, as with the concrete level of learning, parents should continue worksheet activities like this until the student can demonstrate 100% mastery.

Symbolic Level. As the student progresses from pictorial to symbolic learning, the parent will want to use a fading procedure that will help the student learn place value without the use of pictures (i.e., by using only abstract, symbolic numbers). Once more, we suggest that parents develop a series of worksheet activities that require the student to continue circling groups of ten, one hundred, etc. popsicle tally marks. What would change at this level of learning is how the student records the number of ten-groups and one hundred-groups.

Instead of placing a tally mark on a pictured soup can for each ten-group or one hundred-group, prepare a series of worksheets that require the following:

1. Student places tally marks in labeled blanks, instead of pictured cans;
2. Student writes digits, instead of tally marks, in labeled blanks;
3. Student writes digits in unlabeled blanks; and finally
4. Student writes digits alone without labels or blanks.

Alternative Math Strategies

Teaching mathematics to children has traditionally included many rule-driven algorithms. For the most part, these algorithms are verbal in nature and include very few, if any, visual cues or prompts. Classroom teachers typically begin their instruction by demonstrating one or more sample problems, explaining as they go the sequential steps of the algorithm that the student must follow to solve the problem correctly. Students are then expected to memorize the steps.

Consider, for example, the following algorithm for adding fractions with unlike denominators traditionally taught by conventional math teachers:

1. Find the least common denominator (the student must do computation on the side);
2. Divide each given denominator into the new denominator (i.e., the least common denominator discovered in Step 1);
3. Multiply each of these quotients times the corresponding given numerators for the new numerators.
4. Add the two new numerators and bring over this sum for the numerator in the final answer.
5. Bring over the least common denominator as the denominator in the final answer.
6. Simplify your final answer.

Our experience has been that math algorithms like this one, although traditional, are difficult enough for typical students who don't have learning difficulties. But for struggling learners who have language and memory difficulties, however, these traditional algorithms are virtually impossible to master. In fact, many students with learning difficulties will go through most of their upper elementary and junior high school years, never mastering important basic math skills, but nonetheless having to endure teacher after teacher who presents the algorithm with little variety.

One of the best discoveries we made during our years as special education teachers was *alternative math strategies* that were designed for students who have experienced little success learning math through traditional algorithms. These strategies are called *alternative* because they differ radically from the way math problems are typically solved. It has always been interesting, yet mystifying, that after going through years of failure under traditional approaches, students with disabilities will immediately begin showing success with alternative math strategies. We suspect that part of the reason why these strategies work is a phenomenon to which Goldstein alluded when he said, "Sometimes the way to create change is to create a little confusion."[24]

Adding and Subtracting Fractions. Ruais presents a low-stress, alternative math strategy for adding and subtracting common fractions, which he called *Ray Multiplication*.[25] It requires only a few computations to reach a solution. After learning the locational positions of the two numerators and two denominators using pictorial learning and cuing techniques, Ruais recommends that the student be taught to draw three rays (i.e., arrows) in the following manner:

1. from the lower left denominator (LLD) through the upper right numerator (URN);
2. from the lower right denominator (LRD) through the upper left numerator (ULN); and
3. from the lower left denominator (LLD) through the lower right denominator (LRD).

The student is then instructed to multiply the pairs of numbers that fall on each of the three rays and to write the products at the ends of the arrowheads on the rays. At this point, the student has everything he needs to get the final answer. The final denominator is the product that falls on the LLD and LRD ray. The final numerator is the sum (if an addition problem) or difference (if a subtraction problem) of the products on the other two rays. Of course, the final step requires the student to simplify his final fraction if necessary. We provide an example of Ruais' *Ray Multiplication* in Figure 8.3.

Checking Addition. Another alternative math strategy called the *Combined Method* (author unknown) provides a different way to check columnar addition problems. The traditional approach to checking addition requires the student to add vertically in reverse (i.e., if the student adds vertically down the first time, then he will add vertically up for his check). For struggling learners with perceptual and directionality difficulties, checking addition this way can be extremely confusing.

With the *Combined Method*, the student adds all of the digits of an individual addend to get a sum. The student then adds the digits of this sum and continues to add digits in resulting sums until only

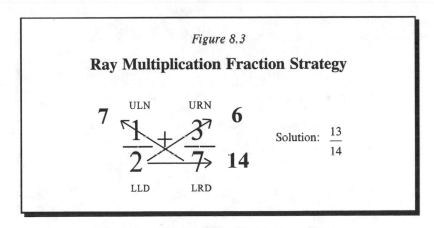

Figure 8.3

Ray Multiplication Fraction Strategy

Solution: $\dfrac{13}{14}$

one digit remains for that addend. For example, if 345 is the addend in an addition problem, the student would add each digit in the addend to yield a sum of 12 (i.e., 3+4+5=12), then each digit in the number 12 is subsequently added to yield a sum of 3 (i.e., 1+2=3). Adding ceases with this addend since 3 is a single digit. This process is done for each of the remaining addends in the problem. The student then adds up all of the single digits that correspond with each of the addends and continues adding until a single digit is reached. We will call this digit X.

Each of the digits in the original sum of the addition problem are also added in similar fashion to get a single digit. We will call this digit Y. The student then compares the two resulting single digits, that is, the digit representing all of the addends (i.e., X) and the digit representing the original sum of the problem (i.e., Y). If the two single digits are an exact match, then the original calculated sum is the correct answer to the problem. Conversely, if the two single digits are not equal matches, then the student made an error in calculating his original sum and must go back and recalculate. We provide an example of the *Combined Method* in Figure 8.4.

There are other alternative math strategies. Since our space is limited, we refer our readers to a book co-authored by Reisman and Kauffman[26] entitled, *Teaching Mathematics to Children with Special Needs*, which may more likely be found at a university library, although local libraries could probably acquire the book through interlibrary loan. This publication contains numerous other alternative strategies like the ones we have illustrated above. *Exceptional*

Figure 8.4

Combined Method for Checking Addition

2 5 7 6 ➤ (add digits in addend) ➤ 2 0 ➤ (add digits) ➤ 2

5 1 5 2 ➤ (add digits in addend) ➤ 1 3 ➤ (add digits) ➤ 4

+ 3 8 4 0 ➤ (add digits in addend) ➤ 1 5 ➤ (add digits) ➤ 6

11, 5 6 8 ➤ (add digits in sum) ➤ 2 1 ➤ (add digits) ➤ 3

The original sum 11,568 is correct since 2 + 4 + 6 = 12, and 1 + 2 = 3, and this 3 matches the 3 derived from adding the digits in the sum.

Diagnostics has also compiled a collection of alternative math strategies that covers the four basic operations, simple fractions, word problems, and metric problems that parents may wish to purchase (see Appendix A for address).

Touch Math Program

The *Touch Math*[27] program is an increasingly popular, commercially-produced, multisensory math remediation program used by conventional educators and private educational clinicians for struggling learners. We believe this program would prove to be both cost effective and successful for parents who have children with skill deficits in addition, subtraction, multiplication, division, number concepts, sequence counting, place value, and shapes and sizes. Bullock describes the program as follows:

Touch Math is aptly named. It takes advantage of the very basic kinesthetic process of touching, plus counting. Each digit has a corresponding number of Touchpoints placed uniformly upon each character.... With the digits 6 through 9, Touchpoints are grouped in two's when appropriate and differentiated graphically with a dot and a concentric circle. Single Touchpoints are touched and counted one time, while double Touchpoints are counted twice. Students are encouraged to count aloud and to follow a uniform touching/counting pattern.[28]

Bullock indicates that it takes first graders about a week to master the correct counting patterns using the *Touch Math* procedure, and that "students introduced to *Touch Math* in later grades normally find it much easier than traditional methods."[29] The program contains a variety of worksheet exercises and practice activities. Scott[30] tested the effectiveness of *Touch Math* recently with learning disabled and mentally retarded children and found that it produced significant gains for these children in the areas of addition and subtraction. See Appendix A for a mailing address and a toll-free number to obtain more information about *Touch Math* plus a free classroom sampler.

Hands-On Equations® Program

Developed and patented in 1986 by Dr. Henry Borenson, a nationally-known mathematics teacher, *Hands-On Equations*® [31] is a commercially-produced, multisensory program. It introduces students to basic algebraic equations (e.g., $4x + 2 = 2x + 10$) by presenting various hands-on activities that follow the concrete, pictorial, and symbolic levels of learning. While requiring no prior knowledge of pre-algebraic skills (e.g., positive and negative numbers, etc.), *Hands-On Equations*® makes use of game pieces which represent the different elements or terms of an algebraic equation. Manipulatives include blue pawns (representing the x-variables), white pawns (representing inverse x's), red number cubes (representing positive integers), and green number cubes (representing negative integers). The student learns how to translate each of the symbolic elements of an equation into its concrete manipulative counterparts, which are balanced on a scale. The scale represents the "=" in the equation.

Hands-On Equations® gently leads the student through a series of 25 lessons that teach him how to make *legal moves*, which allow the student to solve the equation physically, kinesthetically, and intuitively. In addition to providing students of any age with a sound introduction to algebra, other important features of the *Hands-On Equations*® program are that it, "brings success, enjoyment, and fascination to students...enhances student interest in mathematics...[and] does not require [the student to possess] any algebraic prerequisites."[32] Borenson reports that the program may be used as early as third grade with gifted students, fourth grade with average students, and fifth grade for learning disabled students. Borenson has recently developed a video that should assist parents in understanding this technique. See Appendix A for more information.

Computer-Assisted Math

Once more, we refer our readers to the *Special Times*[33] magazine, which reviews different computer software programs that encourage greater learning success in children who struggle. Many of the math programs include features which are educationally appropriate for use with learning disabled children and which parents can manipulate such as auditory-sound, speed-response time, difficulty levels, records of student progress, rewards and reinforcers (e.g., adventure games, printed certificates of excellence, etc.), test creation capability, diagnostic tests, and so forth. Although our list is not exhaustive, we have identified the mathematics computer programs in Figure 8.5 that we believe parents may find most useful. As with other computer software, parents will need to screen these math software programs for objectionable elements.

Other Resources

In addition to the methods we have described above, parents may also be interested in several comprehensive special education methods textbooks used by colleges and universities in preparing special education teachers. Probably the premier methods textbook on the market today for struggling learners is *Teaching Students with Learning Problems.*[34]   An excellent, very practical math methods textbook is *Teaching Mathematics to the Learning Disabled*[35] Finally, we recommend the book, *Teaching Language Arts to Exceptional Children*[36] for special education methods and techniques in the areas of reading, writing, and spelling. Local bookstores should be able to order these books directly from the publishers.

Figure 8.5

Mathematics Computer Software

Title	Grades	Vender	Computers
Bake and Taste	1-9	Mindplay	AP/IBM/MAC
Comparison Kitchen	PreK-3	DLM	AP/IBM
Fraction Action	5-12	Unicorn	AP/IBM/MAC
Integers/Equations	5-10	Hartley	AP/IBM
Math Blaster Plus!	1-8	Davidson	AP/IBM/MAC
Math Concepts	2-8	Hartley	AP/IBM
Math Leap Frog	1-6	Gamco	AP/IBM/MAC
Math Word Problems	4-8	Optimum Res.	AP/IBM
Measure Works	2-6	MECC	AP
Millie's Math House	K-3	Edmark	IBM/MAC
Money	3-8	Gamco	AP/IBM
Place Value 1s,10s,...	3-6	EME	AP/IBM
Primary Word Math	K-5	Milliken	AP/IBM/MAC
Rounding	4-10	Gamco	AP/IBM
Stickybear Numbers	PreK-2	Optimum Res.	AP/IBM
Talking Clock	K-5	Orange Cherry	AP/IBM/MAC
The Coin Changer	K-6	Heartsoft	AP/IBM/MAC
The Calendar	2-8	Gamco	AP/IBM
Using a Calendar	3-6	Hartley	AP/IBM

Note: AP=Apple; MAC=Macintosh

---

[1]Fichter (1993), p. 236
[2]Fernald (1943)
[3]Fernald (1988)
[4]Carbo (1996)
[5]C. Mercer & A. Mercer (1993)
[6]C. Mercer & A. Mercer (1993), p. 465
[7]Kavale & Forness (1987)
[8]Heckelman (1986)
[9]C. Mercer & A. Mercer (1993), p. 467
[10]C. Mercer & A. Mercer (1993), pp. 467-468
[11]Cambridge Development Laboratories (1995, Spring)
[12]Gordon, Vaughn & Schumm (1993)
[13]Fulk & Stormont-Spurgin (1995), p. 17
[14]Gordon, Vaughn & Schumm (1993), p. 178
[15]Goldstein (1989)
[16]Gordon, Vaughn & Schumm (1993), p. 179
[17]Wong (1986), p. 172

[18]Wong (1986), p. 172
[19]Gordon, Vaughn & Schumm (1993), p. 179
[20]Graham & Freeman (1985)
[21]Cambridge Development Laboratories (1995, Spring)
[22]Keller & J. Sutton (1992)
[23]C. Mercer & A. Mercer (1993)
[24]Goldstein (1989)
[25]Ruais (1978)
[26]Reisman & S. H. Kauffman (1981)
[27]Bullock (1994)
[28]Bullock (1992), p. 121
[29]Bullock (1992), p. 121
[30]Scott (1993)
[31]Borenson (1994)
[32]The Hands-On Equations Learning System brochure (no date)
[33]Cambridge Development Laboratories (1995, Spring)
[34]C. Mercer & A. Mercer (1993)
[35]Bley & Thornton (1995)
[36]Wallace, Cohen, & Polloway (1987)

9

Teaching Study Skills

Students learn through *intentional* and *incidental* instruction.[1] Intentional instruction occurs when teachers teach skills directly through presentations, discussions, and the like. Incidental instruction occurs when students acquire skills on their own through independent study, self-instruction, or by simply imitating others. While average learners typically learn study skills incidentally, it has been our experience as special educators that struggling learners do not. They have to be intentionally taught study skills such as memorizing, outlining, test-taking, and so on.

We devote this chapter, then, to techniques that parents may use to teach study skills directly to their struggling learners. For additional ideas, parents may wish to peruse a comprehensive listing of study skill resources for students with disabilities provided by Cronin and Currie[2] (see reference list).

Study Habits Survey

Helping a struggling learner pinpoint his study skill weaknesses and become more aware of those weaknesses is a prerequisite to study skill instruction. One of the best informal assessment instruments available is the *How Am I Doing? Study Habits Questionnaire* by Bragstad and Stumpf[3] (See Figure 9.1). The questionnaire consists of 50 self-assessment questions that cover several major study skill areas including concentration, remembering, organizing time, studying textbook chapters, listening and taking notes, taking tests, and motivation. An answer key and a section for categorizing study skill strengths and weaknesses is provided at the end of the instrument. Parents may need to read the items to struggling learners who have reading difficulties.

Self-Monitoring for Attention

Many struggling learners, particularly LD and ADD students, typically have problems coming to or maintaining attention and staying on-task. One of the most popular treatments for severe attention problems is drug therapy, that is, the use of psycho-stimulant drugs such as Ritalin, Cimetidine, Dexedrine, etc. Although taking a drug for attention problems is easy and convenient for both parents and child, the research on its effectiveness is presently mixed.

For example, Swanson and his colleagues[4] have reviewed available studies and concluded that use of psycho-stimulant medication produces only *temporary* management and improvement of behavior problems typically associated with attention deficit disorder. More important, drug therapy generally results in "frequent problems with eating and sleeping" with "no significant improvement in reading skills...athletic or game skills...positive social skills...[and] no improvement in academic achievement."[5] Yet Barkley,[6] in a summary of recent research on the efficacy of drug therapy, reports that about 92% of ADD students (inattention subtype) on medication show improvement, and approximately 50% are completely normalized (i.e., cured).

Our position, like Short's, is that children with attention difficulties "[do] not have to be treated with drugs as many school children are."[7] But for those students who have persistent, more severe attention difficulties, parents would be wise to consider drug therapy only as a last resort after behavioral approaches alone have been exhausted[8] and with the condition that behavioral techniques will continue (see Chapter 10 for behavioral techniques). We concur with

Figure 9.1

How Am I Doing?
(Study Habits Questionnaire)

Name_____Date_____

The purpose of this questionnaire is to help you get information about how you study right now. As you examine the results, you will discover your areas of strength and weakness. The results will have meaning only if you are honest and respond as accurately as possible. If the statement is true about you, circle Y for yes. If the statement is false as it applies to you, circle N for no. Be sure to circle Y or N for each statement. Answer carefully so that you get accurate information.

1. I have trouble finishing tests on time.   Y   N

2. I set aside a regular time for studying every day.   Y   N

3. Before I read a chapter, I turn headings into questions so   Y   N
   that I know what I'm going to learn.

4. I don't have much luck following a definite study schedule.   Y   N

5. I give up if an assignment is difficult.   Y   N

6. I have difficulty determining important points in lessons.   Y   N

7. Before class starts, I review yesterday's lesson notes.   Y   N

8. I waste time because I am not organized.   Y   N

9. I focus entirely on my work when I study.   Y   N

10. I feel uncomfortable reading a chapter unless I've read all   Y   N
    the headings and the summary first.

11. I don't bother taking notes during lessons.   Y   N

12. I get sleepy when I study.   Y   N

13. I check my lesson notes to fill in any missed words soon   Y   N
    after the lesson.

14. I seldom hear a lesson that is well organized.   Y   N

15. I enjoy learning.   Y   N

16. Before I begin an assignment, I estimate how long it will   Y   N
    take me and then try to beat the clock.

17. Before answering an essay question, I organize what I am   Y   N
    going to write.

Adapted from *How Am I Doing? (Study Habits Questionnaire)* in *A Guidebook for Teaching Study Skills and Motivation* (2nd ed.) by Bernice Jensen Bragstad and Sharyn Mueller Stumpf (1987), pp. 203-205, Allyn & Bacon, Inc. Reprinted by permission.

18. I have difficulty concentrating when I study.   Y   N

19. Using lesson notes and the textbook, I can usually predict   Y   N
50-60 percent of the questions on a test.

20. I could get better grades.   Y   N

21. I take time to study every day.   Y   N

22. I try to record everything my teacher says in a lesson.   Y   N

23. I set aside time every week to review for each class.   Y   N

24. Every time I study for a class, I spend some time in   Y   N
review.

25. I'd rather get through fast than have a perfect paper.   Y   N

26. I usually lose points on my tests because of careless   Y   N
mistakes.

27. I usually seek a quiet place to study.   Y   N

28. Before I leave class, I make sure that I know what   Y   N
homework to do and how to do it.

29. I have a hard time getting interested in some of my classes.   Y   N

30. Good grades are important to me.   Y   N

31. I stop to recite what I remember after reading each section   Y   N
in a chapter.

32. I know what time of day I do my best studying.   Y   N

33. I study only when I feel like it.   Y   N

34. I seldom read the questions at the end of the chapter before   Y   N
I begin reading the chapter.

35. I often have trouble finding enough time to study.   Y   N

36. I remember little of what I study.   Y   N

37. I put off studying that I should be doing.   Y   N

38. To remember better, I check main headings and the   Y   N
summary before I read a chapter or article.

39. Tests make me so nervous that I can't do my best.   Y   N

40. I wait until the night before a test to review my lesson notes.   Y   N

41. I listen carefully in a lesson but I do not take notes.   Y   N

42. I take time to review the chapter soon after I read it.   Y   N

Adapted from *How Am I Doing? (Study Habits Questionnaire)* in *A Guidebook for Teaching Study Skills and Motivation* (2nd ed.) by Bernice Jensen Bragstad and Sharyn Mueller Stumpf (1987), pp. 203-205, Allyn & Bacon, Inc. Reprinted by permission.

43. I really "dig in" when I study.   Y   N
44. Before starting a test, I plan how much time to use on each   Y   N
    section of the test.
45. I spend too much time on some subjects and not enough on   Y   N
    others.
46. I skip over charts, graphs, and tables when I read a chapter.   Y   N
47. I find it difficult to know what is important in a chapter.   Y   N
48. If I have any time left, I check over my test to avoid errors.   Y   N
49. Because I want to remember, I listen carefully to any   Y   N
    explanations during lessons.
50. Daydreaming interferes with my studying.   Y   N

Answer Key: How Am I Doing?

1. N	11. N	21. Y	31. Y	41. N
2. Y	12. N	22. N	32. Y	42. Y
3. Y	13. Y	23. Y	33. N	43. Y
4. N	14. N	24. Y	34. N	44. Y
5. N	15. Y	25. N	35. N	45. N
6. N	16. Y	26. N	36. N	46. N
7. Y	17. Y	27. Y	37. N	47. N
8. N	18. N	28. Y	38. Y	48. Y
9. Y	19. Y	29. N	39. N	49. Y
10. Y	20. Y	30. Y	40. N	50. N

What Are My Strengths and Weaknesses? [Circle all missed items.]

Concentration		9	12	16	18	27	33	50
Remembering		23	24	29	36	38	40	49
Organizing time		2	4	8	21	32	35	45
Studying a chapter		3	10	31	34	42	46	47
Listening and taking notes		6	7	11	13	14	22	41
Taking tests		1	17	19	26	39	44	48
Motivation	5	15	20	25	28	30	37	43

Adapted from *How Am I Doing? (Study Habits Questionnaire)* in *A Guidebook for Teaching Study Skills and Motivation* (2nd ed.) by Bernice Jensen Bragstad and Sharyn Mueller Stumpf (1987), pp. 203–205, Allyn & Bacon, Inc. Reprinted by permission.

Strayer who holds that the "use of drugs with our children...[should] not [be] a first or third or fourth choice of treatment. It comes about last on the list..."[9]

Drug therapy is not the only approach that can be used to help children who have attention problems. Other inexpensive, non-pharmacological approaches have been found to be effective. For example, a technique called *self-monitoring* equips children with the skills they need to regulate and evaluate their own on-task behavior. Hallahan and his colleagues have concluded that self-monitoring "works best when attention is the primary problem."[10] We believe that teaching a child to monitor his own behavior is an ultimate goal of every Christian parent and teacher. In addition to helping children control their attention, self-monitoring should assist children, once they become adults, in being independent in many life skills and behaviors.

Self-monitoring for attention is a technique that makes use of a continuous-play audiotape with random tones that helps a child stay on-task during class time, seatwork or independent study without continual intervention by the parent. This technique can also be used to help children attend better to the parent's verbal instruction. Using an earphone or headphone set and a standard tape player, the child is cued audibly by beeps on the tape, which occur randomly at 15- to 120-second intervals. The child is instructed to ask himself at each beep, "Was I paying attention to my work (or the teacher)?" The child then marks either "yes" or "no" on an accompanying check sheet. Wrist counters, print-out-style calculators, and grocery counters can also be used as recording instruments. Parents will need to train their youngster in self-questioning and in using the self-monitoring tape.

It is important in self-monitoring to set an attention goal for the child. The initial goal can be established by calculating the average of the percentages of "yes" responses on the first week's worth of check sheets. The "yes" goal can then be increased gradually across school weeks. Parents may increase the power of this technique by issuing appropriate rewards and reinforcers[11] contingent upon the student meeting the pre-determined success goal.

It might be good to use self-monitoring sparingly in the beginning. This technique is highly structured and students may resist having to account for their attention so frequently. There may be less resistance, however, if parents carefully choose reinforcers and rewards that the child strongly desires (refer to Chapter 10 on how to select appropriate reinforcers). Once a child's attention span has increased to an acceptable level using self-monitoring, the various elements of the technique can be faded out or weaned away, one at a time (the audiotape first, then the check sheet or recording device). Reintroduce either or both of these two elements when attention skills show signs of waning.

Parents can make their own self-monitoring audiotape for use in the home or purchase an inexpensive commercially-produced version developed by Dr. Harvey Parker[12] which is available from the ADD Warehouse in Florida. Dr. Parker's kit includes the audiotape, a pack of check sheets, and an instruction manual for approximately $20. A free catalog describing Parker's self-monitoring program, along with books and other non-drug products for children with attention problems can be ordered by calling ADD Warehouse's toll-free number (see Appendix A).

Outlining

Outlining is an important study skill for two major reasons. One, it helps struggling learners identify essential ideas in reading passages. Two, outlining clarifies difficult reading passages. It provides a way to simplify content that may be challenging to students with disabilities. As a study technique, outlining can be used in any academic subject such as literature, science, and history where skills and content are absorbed through reading.

Hierarchical outlining is the traditional form of outlining. Most parents are familiar with this type. Main topics, subtopics, and corresponding details that relate to a certain theme or incident are organized by Roman numerals (i.e., I, II, III, etc.), capital letters, and lowercase letters, respectively. Parents who choose to use hierarchical outlining must ensure that struggling learners know Roman numerals up to ten and that they can differentiate between capital and lowercase letters. Providing a template sheet where the Roman numerals, and capital and lowercase letters are prearranged with open space for the student to fill-in outline material would be a good way to begin teaching hierarchical outlining.

The heavy verbal emphasis may prevent some struggling learners from responding well to hierarchical outlining, particularly if they have learning disabilities in reading or written expression. In Figure 9.2, we provide other outlining techniques that parents and students may find useful that were adapted from Giordano.[13]

Figure 9.2

Outlining Techniques

Type	Description
● Pictorial outlining	Student makes sketches or illustrations with a minimum number of strokes to represent details and arranges them in sequence.
● Topical outlining	Student identifies a central topic or theme and records details randomly in list format that relate to the topic, e.g., reporter's notebook.
● Charting	Student arranges details in sequence that have to do with a time period or are spatial in nature, e.g., use of time lines, concentric circles, or matrices.
● Question sets	Student responds to a set of questions that require him to pull critical information from the passage, e.g., Who? What? Where? When? Why? and so on.
● Array outlining	Student identifies the central character in a story and actions. The name of the character is placed in a circle and actions, briefly worded, are fanned around the circle. Arrows from the circle to the action indicate character was initiator; arrows from actions to the circle indicate character was recipient.

Adapted from Giordano, G. (1984). *Teaching writing to LD students*. Rockville, MD: Aspen.

Memorizing

In our work with families, many have asked for ideas on how to help the struggling learner who has memory deficits. It would be awfully tempting to just recommend one of the exorbitantly priced memory improvement programs advertised on radio and television and be done with it. However, we have yet to see any experimental studies that definitively prove the effectiveness of these quick and easy programs with children who have learning difficulties. Therefore, we will refrain from recommending them at all. In addition, while some early studies are showing that the drug, Ampricon will improve memory in older men with Alzheimer's disease,[14] parents should be cautious in generalizing effects to young children.

What we do know is that various memory recall techniques, when used consistently, can help children perform better on learning tasks that require them to retrieve information that they have committed to memory. The best collection of memory techniques that we are aware of has been compiled by Greenbaum.[15] Although these memory techniques were recommended in the context of improving spelling performance, we believe these ideas can be used quite effectively in memorizing information in other academic areas. Greenbaum suggests that memorization can be enhanced by the following activities:

- Say or vocalize the item to be memorized, but vary voice sound (e.g., from whispering, to shouting, to singing, etc.);
- Emphasize or exaggerate vocally the difficult parts of the item to be memorized;
- Speak the elements (e.g., letters, digits) while writing them;
- Highlight with color the difficult parts;
- Underline difficult parts;
- Vary the lettering font or style when writing difficult parts (e.g., switch from print to cursive, or choose different letter font if using a computer or word processor);
- Vary the lettering size when writing difficult parts (e.g., switch from mix of upper and lower case to all upper case, or choose a different point type if using a word computer or word processor);

- Use tactile letters or digits, but vary with difficult parts (e.g., switch from plastic or wood items to sandpaper);
- Vary writing surface and/or writing channel (e.g., chalkboard, whiteboard, manual typewriter, computer keyboard, writing in sand, writing on carpeting or floor); and
- Use finger tracing activities (e.g., over written words/ digits).

Monitoring Errors

COPS is an error-monitoring strategy for writing developed by Ellis and Lenz.[16] Each letter in the mnemonic prompts the student to check his writing for a specific type of error before turning in his paper to be graded:

C = Have I capitalized the first word and all proper nouns?
O = How is the overall appearance?
P = Have I used end punctuation, commas, and semicolons correctly?
S = Do the words look like they are spelled right...?

The COPS strategy would be applicable to any subject where written assignments are required, not just English classes.

Completing Assignments

Robinson[17] developed an assignment completion strategy called, AWARE, that requires the student to set goals and self-evaluate his performance. The student records his responses to five self-evaluation questions on a grid, each corresponding to a letter in the word, "AWARE" (See Figure 9.3).

Responses to "A" and "W" are recorded on the grid prior to beginning the assignment or project. The next two responses to "A" and "R" are recorded on the grid by the student immediately after completion of the assignment. The final response, "E," is recorded after the teacher grades the assignment. The teacher should discuss with the student any discrepancies between his self-evaluation (i.e., his ratings for "A," "W," "A," and "R") and the teacher evaluation (i.e., "E") of the project.

Figure 9.3

Assignment Completion Strategy

Assignment	A	W	A	R	E
1.					
2.					
3.					
4.					

A = Ask yourself what grade you want to earn [i.e., A, B, etc., or 100%, 90%, etc.]. Put the score in the box labeled A.

W = WORK-Note...how much time you think it will take to complete the assignment.

A = Assignment completed? Check yes or no.

R = Rate your effort. What score do you think your teacher will give you?

E — End result. What score did you receive?[18]

Source: Robinson, S. (1987). Self-management: A tool for independence—A means of motivation. *LD Forum, 12,* 11-13.

Taking Tests

Carman and Adams[19] developed a test-taking strategy, SCORER, that is taught universally by special educators. SCORER should be used primarily when taking objective-type tests (i.e., multiple choice, true/false, etc. items). Each letter in SCORER cues the student to remember an important test-taking principle:

S = Schedule your time.
C = Look for clue words.
O = Omit difficult questions [i.e., postpone briefly].
R = Read carefully.
E = Estimate your answers.
R = Review your work [making sure to remember omitted items]...

The SCORER strategy can be adapted for use with essay, short answer, or open-ended question tests; however, we believe it would be more beneficial for parents to teach the following test-taking skills for use with subjective tests:

- Make sure the student understands the different testing terms such as *compare, contrast, illustrate, briefly describe, define, elaborate,* and so on.
- Train the student to memorize main points of topics and issues from notes and outlines of material that he will be tested over for possible use as a skeletal outline on essay items.
- Train the student to turn his test upside down prior to beginning and jot down memorized points in case a panic attack (i.e., memory lapse) occurs unexpectedly.
- Train the student to set aside 1/4 to 1/3 of his allocated test time per essay item for thinking and organization of thoughts only—no writing.

Managing Time

Productivity and *efficiency* in school work can be just as important as *accuracy*. Unfortunately, getting assignments done in a timely manner, which fosters productivity and efficiency, tends to take a back seat many times to accuracy, if it has a place in some educational programs at all. While encouraging a student to, "Take your time, and be careful," may increase accuracy to some degree, there is a point when taking too much time causes productivity and efficiency to suffer. Nonetheless, getting struggling learners ready to compete in this world, and moreover, to be successful, will require that they do their assigned tasks well (i.e., accuracy) and within the expected time frame (i.e., efficiency). Parents of struggling learners, then, will need to include teaching time management in their repertoire of study techniques.

Time Awareness

We believe that teaching time awareness is a prerequisite to teaching time management. Struggling learners must first be aware of how much time they have available to complete specific tasks. Parents can increase time awareness by using timers and stopwatches when they require school assignments. For example, one mother set the timer for 12 minutes to allow her son to read a brief passage in his literature book and answer 7 comprehension questions afterwards (of course, the number of minutes would vary depending on a student's reading rate). If students successfully complete their required assignments in the allocated time period, parents should reward them for both accuracy and efficiency.

Time Management

Time management should revolve around four goals, which students can easily remember through the mnemonic, COBA:

C = Complete assignments on time
O = Organize your environment for study
B – Balance extracurricular activities and required study
A – Allocate sufficient time for major assignments and projects

Teaching time management begins by externally monitoring the student's time through *adult-mediated* strategies. Once the student shows efficiency in school work with adult-mediated strategies, parents should then arrange *peer mediated* strategies. The final stage of teaching time management allows the student to monitor himself through *self-mediated* time management strategies.

Visual reminders are one example of an adult mediated strategy. Placing posters in strategic places in the home classroom that display time management slogans work very well. Bliss,[20] for example, identifies a number of time management slogans including, "Be a doer not a dawdler," "Winners don't wait," "Due tomorrow: Do today!" "Do the worst first," "Do it anyway!" and so on. Other adult-mediated strategies are assignment books, date books, electronic calendars, and so on that should be monitored and checked regularly by the parent.

Finally, as students mature and show time management success with adult-mediated strategies, parents can make use of older brothers and sisters or close friends in developing peer-mediated strategies. For example, a buddy system would allow a struggling learner's best friend to call him each afternoon on the phone (limit to 5 minutes only for monitoring assignments) and ask a series of questions regarding the extent to which school assignments have been completed.

Self-mediated time management strategies may include checklists that break down tasks into individual substeps that the struggling learner can check-off as he completes them in a given time frame. As with adult-mediated strategies, success with peer-mediated and self-mediated time management strategies should be rewarded appropriately.

----

[1]Luftig (1987)
[2]Cronin & Currie (1984)
[3]Bragstad & Stumpf (1987), pp. 203-205
[4]Swanson, McBurnett, Wigal, Pfiffner, Lerner, M. A., Williams, Christian, Tamm, Willicutt, Crowley, Clevenger, Khouzam, Woo, Crinella, & Fisher (1993)
[5]Swanson et al. (1993), p. 159
[6]Barkley (1996)
[7]Short (1994), p. 39
[8]J. Sutton (1994d)
[9]Strayer (1994), p. 1
[10]Hallahan, Hall, Ianna, Kneedler, Lloyd, Loper, & Reeve (1983), p. 104
[11]Parker (1992)
[12]Parker (1990)
[13]Giordano (1984)
[14]CBS Radio News, 11-17-96
[15]Greenbaum (1987)
[16]Ellis & Lenz (1987)
[17]Robinson (1987)
[18]Robinson (1987), pp. 11-13
[19]Carman & Adams (1972)
[20]Bliss (1983)

Chapter

10

Managing Behavior

A ll children misbehave at times. For students with disabilities, however, undesirable behavior occurs more often.
In addition to problems that stem from their sin natures, disabled
students have characteristic, symptomatic behavior problems that generally accompany their disabilities (See Chapter 1). Managing student behavior, then, is a skill that is important for all parents, but
perhaps more so for those who have struggling learners. C. Michael
Nelson,[1] maintains that unless teachers effectively manage student
behavior, optimal, effective learning probably will not occur. It stands
to reason, that parents of struggling learners will maximize their home
teaching efforts if they make behavior management techniques an
integral part of their educational programs.

We begin this chapter with a discussion of some *preventative*
techniques. Next we present several *short-term* behavior management techniques that can be implemented on the spot when problem
behaviors are first observed. We conclude with a number of *long-
term* techniques for behaviors in children that are slow at developing
and improving. Appendix A provides a number of resources on behavior management that parents may find useful.

Preventative Techniques

We can prevent certain problems in our lives by exercising proper precautions. For example, mechanics admonish us to change the oil regularly in our automobiles in order to prevent major breakdowns in the engine. As responsible drivers, we must be careful to check the tires on our cars to make sure they have adequate tread so that needless accidents will not occur during rainy or icy weather. There are numerous other preventative checks to which we must give attention as we operate vehicles. If we fail to implement these preventative measures, we should expect accidents and mechanical problems to occur more often.

It is much the same with our health. We are told repeatedly by physicians and health authorities that we should keep our weight down, exercise consistently, take vitamins, have regular physical checkups, and so on. If we are careful to address these precautions, we are less likely to experience more serious, potentially life-threatening health problems later on such as heart attacks and certain forms of cancer.

Similarly, parents will need to implement preventative techniques in order to head off some problem behaviors in children. W. Camp and B. Camp[2] discuss a number of preventative behavior management techniques. Five in particular are helpful to parents who have struggling learners.

Set up your classroom to encourage good behavior. It is imperative that parents consider where they will provide instruction for their children. It will be awfully tempting to allow children to do their school work in any room in the house, even the family room or bedroom. But for children with disabilities, it is important to provide an instructional environment that is highly structured, free from distracting stimuli, and conducive to learning and good behavior (see Chapter 5).

Parents may want to consider setting up a room in the home that will be used exclusively for school. Comfortable desks, tables, and chairs should be available for children to do their work. Use small white boards or chalk boards for providing direct instruction. File cabinets or cubby holes can be used for organizing and storing workbooks and materials. These types of things will provide the necessary structure that children with disabilities need to learn and behave optimally.

Start lessons promptly. We have discussed in Chapter 5 the necessity of developing a daily routine and schedule with predetermined times for instruction, independent work, and so on. We believe that a very important preventative behavior technique is starting each activity on the daily schedule promptly.

The old adage, "Idleness is the devil's workshop" immediately comes to mind for most parents. We must recognize that when we fail to start an activity on time, we may be inviting our children to misbehave or think about misbehaving. Some parents may downplay the importance of this preventative technique by arguing that a few minutes will not make that much difference. But, oh, how it can! How much time does a child need to get up from his assigned place and begin meandering around the home or outside in the yard? We need to assist struggling learners as much as possible in maintaining their concentration and attention. As we start class on time and abide rigidly to the daily schedule, we can expect fewer distractions and behavior problems.

Tolerate some noise and movement. Some parents may grapple initially with this preventative technique. After all, our children should be perfectly quiet and still, right? This is simply not the case with children who have disabilities. We have discussed in Chapter 1 some of the accompanying behavior characteristics of children with disabilities. For example, we know that many disabled children will demonstrate excessive movement (i.e., hyperactivity) at times. They will tend to talk out at times without permission, because they may lack appropriate self-control skills.

While our goal is to reduce movement and talk out problems in our disabled children as much as possible, we probably will not get these noise and movement problems down to zero rates. We are not suggesting that parents excuse away noise and movement problems altogether. What we are saying is that we cannot expect perfection from children who have obvious, God-given imperfections and limitations in their learning and behavior. Parents are wise to exercise a reasonable degree of tolerance.

Keep behavior rules simple and clear. We recommend that home teachers consider these three ideas:

1. Develop four to six behavior rules, stated in positive, age-appropriate terms and using as few words as possible;
2. Write them on poster board in flamboyant, attractive colors; and
3. Post them in a strategic position where the student looks frequently.

The choice of behavior rules will vary based on the needs of the child. It is most important, though, that parents use wording that is brief and understandable to the child. Although "Remain seated unless you have permission to get up" is appropriate and brief enough for students in middle school grades, the wording is probably too long and lofty for elementary-age students. Two simple words, "Stay seated," may be better for them. For nonreaders and younger children, you may have to use picture rules.

The place to post the behavior rules is critical. We recall one conventional classroom teacher who was extremely selective in choosing the best place. Instead of arbitrarily posting the rules just anywhere in the classroom, she observed for several days to determine where her students would look the most when they were not engaged in their school work. She concluded that the ideal place was the little window on the classroom door, since this was where her students would often look to see if any of their friends were passing in the hallway. Another teacher determined the best strategic position was near the clock on the front classroom wall.

Enforce behavior rules consistently. This can be a difficult preventative technique to implement for any teacher. Most parents have problems in consistently living right themselves, let alone insuring their children are behaving well on a regular basis. Although we will probably not catch every behavior rule infraction that our children commit, we need to be as consistent as possible in enforcing the rules that we have set up in the home.

Children with disabilities have more problems with consistent school performance than their nondisabled counterparts. It stands to reason that, in order to assist them in behaving consistently, parents will need to provide continual enforcement of behavior expectations. The more consistent we are at requiring these children to be responsible and accountable for behaving well, the greater the chance they will generalize good behavior in the years to come as they grow older and mature. As a preventative technique, we are reducing the probability that more serious behavior problems will ensue in the future if we consistently enforce basic behavioral rules along the way.

Short-term Techniques

These techniques are also referred to as *antiseptic* or *band-aid* approaches to managing student behavior. We call them *short-term* techniques for two reasons. First, they are short-term with regard to the amount of advanced preparation necessary for the home teacher to get the technique ready for use and implementation. Once the parent has mastered an understanding of these techniques, she only need exercise keen observation and memory retrieval skills in knowing when to implement a certain short-term technique.

Finally, these techniques are short-term because the home teacher will not have to wait a long time (e.g., from several weeks to several months) to see the desired change in behavior. For the most part, if the undesired behavior is minor in nature (e.g., tapping pencil on desk) and not too deep seated, the parent should expect the behavior to change right on the spot, or within a brief time period, provided the short-term techniques are applied appropriately, confidently, and firmly.

Parents should consider implementing short-term techniques at the earliest occurrence, better yet at the onset of problem behaviors. One additional thing to keep in mind is that one short-term technique used alone may not be enough to get a problem behavior under control. Parents may need to implement several short-term techniques in succession with a single behavior infraction in order to see successful behavior change.

It is also important not to discount the effectiveness of any one short-term technique just because it may not seem effective on a particular day. Parents may need to apply a technique on a number of different days in order to see the full effect. How long a parent should apply short-term techniques will vary based on the nature of the problem and the severity of the child's disability. Parents should exhaust short-term techniques before implementing more time-consuming and intensive long-term behavior management techniques. Consider the following short-term techniques.

Planned Ignoring With Praise. For minor classroom problem behaviors, simply ignoring the misbehavior while concurrently praising the child for something that he is doing right works many times. Parents should expect the problem behavior to diminish soon thereafter. An explanation of why this short-term technique works is somewhat difficult. But it may well be that the child is so taken aback that he has been praised for doing some seemingly menial task or behavior well (e.g., sitting straight in his chair) that he forgets about the minor problem behavior in which he was engaged.

Imagine a young boy sitting at his desk (obviously in deep thought and reflection over his school work!) and incessantly tapping his pencil. It is not unusual for typical teachers who have very low tolerance for any noise or movement to reprimand a boy like this. In experimental studies, it has been shown that ignoring troublesome behaviors like pencil tapping while praising the student for doing something well is effective in causing the problem behavior to diminish.[3] R. Hall and M. Hall[4] provide additional guidelines on how to use planned ignoring.

Proximity Control. There will be times when parents may need to leave a child alone momentarily to work independently on a school assignment. The average, self-motivated child generally stays on-task and remains undistracted. Students with disabilities, however, typically get off-task very quickly when left alone, and behavior problems inevitably ensue.

A good way to get behavior back under control is for the parent to re-enter the room where the child was left alone to work and move near the student by positioning her body next to the child, that is, in *close proximity* to the child. The mere presence of an adult being near the student is enough to cause him to pause and consider his unacceptable behavior and desist. No doubt the maturity, control, and authority of a parent has a positive influence and plays a big part in the immediate behavior change of a child.

We see proximity control used often by highway patrolmen. It is not uncommon to see drivers on a freeway speeding upwards to 65 or 70 miles per hour, not abiding by the posted speed limit. Amazingly, these drivers will immediately reduce their speed at the mere sight of a highway patrol car in the general locale. We should expect to see the same type of behavior change in our children as we apply proximity control in the home.

Urge to Self-reflect. Parents should not assume that all inappropriate behavior in disabled children stems from their sin natures. Some inappropriate and undesirable behaviors are characteristic symptoms of the disability itself, for example, shoddy penmanship for learning disabled students or failure to concentrate in children with attention deficit disorder. Many times parents forget that struggling learners are not mature adults and may not always remember *why* or *how* they are to behave properly. For children with disabilities, who may indeed have short- or long-term memory problems, possibly even reasoning difficulties, times of inappropriate behavior may come more often.

The *urge to self-reflect* technique calls for the parent to go through a series of oral questions with the child. The number of oral questions will vary from one child to another and from one situation to the next. But the phrasing of each question should cause the child to pause and *reflect* momentarily on the inappropriateness of his actions or behavior. The series of questions should gradually lead the child to reconsider his behavior and improve.

Consider Janie, an elementary mildly mentally disabled young girl, who has doodled all over her math worksheet. Janie's mother immediately notices the messy work and, while pointing to the doodled marks, asks her daughter these questions: "Are you pleased with how your paper looks?...Do you think this is appropriate?...Is this paper neat?... Do you remember what we learned yesterday about neat school papers?...How could you make this paper look neater?" Parents should prompt the child to give a clear "yes" or "no" response to each question. Even if the parent has to go through the entire series of questions, it should take no more than a couple of minutes.

Humor as a tension diffuser. No doubt there will be times during the school day when the pressure of school work seems almost unbearable to children with disabilities. They may lose their good attitudes and composure. Tempers may flare. Such occasions can be short-lived, though, if parents understand how and when to use *humor as a tension diffuser.*

Imagine a young learning disabled girl, Jenelle, who has been working on trying to master her three spelling words for the day. She has been at it for 45 minutes. Her mother gives her a quiz to check her mastery, and Jenelle only gets 2 of 3 correct. Jenelle understands from a prior agreement with her mother that she has to continue re-petitively writing and practicing each of the three required spelling words until all three can be written correctly at one quizzing. Jenelle's temper gets the better of her, and she begins grumbling, complain-ing, and finally just pouts. Jenelle's mother smiles at her lovingly and in a very light-hearted manner says to her, "Sweetie...you look as blown-up as a bullfrog!" at which time Jenelle bursts into joyful laughter. The mother's act of using humor in this situation was a quick, on-the-spot way of breaking the tension of the moment and may have prevented Jenelle's minor behavior from escalating into a more serious problem.

Long-term Techniques

We call these techniques that follow *long-term* techniques for the opposite reasons that we called the prior ones *short-term*. First, long-term techniques require the parent to invest considerable more time thinking, planning, and preparing for implementation. Second, these techniques are viewed as long-term with respect to the amount of time a parent will have to wait for behavior to change. For ex-ample, waiting from several weeks to several months for long-term techniques to take effect would not be unusual. There are two major types of behavior management techniques that we will discuss in the paragraphs that follow—*enhancement* techniques and *reduction* tech-niques. Each reflects a different goal of behavior change.

Enhancement Techniques

We use enhancement techniques to *increase* the rate of or main-tain good, desirable, appropriate behaviors in our children. When a child does not do enough of a good behavior (e.g., correctly solving math problems, knowing how to ask appropriately for something), enhancement techniques should be implemented to help him learn how to do it more often. A common thread that runs throughout many of the enhancement techniques is *positive reinforcement*. Ac-cording to Axelrod,[5] positive reinforcement is the most powerful strat-egy in managing behavior. When teachers give children rewards and positive consequences in response to appropriate behavior, they are delivering positive reinforcement. Yet we will see later that positive reinforcers can also be withheld from a child for the purpose of re-ducing inappropriate behavior.

Positive Reinforcement Programs   The simplest of all the enhancement techniques to develop and implement, positive reinforcement programs call for the teacher to reward the child for doing more of a desirable behavior or skill (e.g., completing 10 math problems in 15 minutes instead of 5) or performing the skill with better proficiency (e.g., getting 90% accuracy on a set of math problems instead of 75%). Choosing the right types of reinforcers that are appropriate to the child's maturity level and ones for which he has a strong desire is key to the success of a positive reinforcement program.

Types of Reinforcers. There are six types of reinforcers that students will respond to during their formative years: tactile-sensory (e.g., cuddling, hugs, etc.), edible, tangible, token, activity, and social reinforcers. We should expect younger children to desire and respond primarily to tactile-sensory, edible, and tangible forms of reinforcers since they are more extrinsic and materialistic in nature. Yet we should expect older students and adults to respond more favorably to token, activity, and social types of reinforcers most of the time.

Social reinforcers are the highest level of reinforcer. As such, we should not expect chronologically or developmentally younger children to be sufficiently reinforced from only a verbal comment such as "Good work!" when they do well. Younger children are generally not mature enough to receive the subtle reinforcing effect of social reinforcers. However, we should expect older, more mature and independent functioning adults to respond to social reinforcers. For example, a supervisor on a job site should expect a subordinate worker to continue performing quality work upon receiving encouraging words such as "Good job!" from the supervisor. Although the worker receives token reinforcement (i.e., a paycheck) intermittently along the way, he doesn't need to receive his wages by the day (or the hour) in order to keep on working at optimal levels. The social reinforcer from his boss is enough for the moment.

In order for parents to prepare children to be able to receive and respond to social reinforcers in the future, however, they will need to combine a social reinforcer such as "Good work on those spelling words!" with a lower order reinforcer such as an edible, tangible, token, and activity reinforcer. If we do this consistently through the years, we should expect children to be able to respond favorably to social reinforcers alone when they reach adulthood. Our God, in a similar way, showers us with rich blessings while here on this earth, yet we will one day be expected to respond in a spiritually mature way to His words, "Well done, thou good and faithful servant" (Matt. 25:21).

We regret that Christian parents and teachers are sometimes reluctant to reward children for good behavior for fear that they may spoil them. Some believe simply that, "Doing right is its own reward." Perhaps to the great surprise of many, there is little, if any, Scriptural support for this position, nor is it in keeping with God's example to us in the Bible. When it comes to appropriate spiritual behavior, "Doing right will earn you a reward" is the more accurate message taught in God's Word. I Corinthians 3:14 tells us, "If any man's work abide which he hath built thereupon, he shall receive a reward."

A careful look into the Scripture reveals that God is a liberal Giver of reinforcers and rewards (i.e., blessings) to His children. In fact, the richer blessings from God were always contingent upon obedience to His Word. God made provision for a number of different types of reinforcers and blessings in Scripture, including *edible* rewards ("manna" in Ex. 16:4 and "harvest" in Gen. 8:22), *tangible* and *token* rewards ("spoil" in Prov. 1:13), activity rewards ("rest" in Lev. 26:34), and social reinforcers ("help meet" in Gen. 2:18; "companions" in Phil. 2:25; and "friends" in Prov. 18:24). We believe, therefore, based on God's example, that parents should give rewards and reinforcers freely and frequently to children upon demonstration of good behavior.

Reinforcement Survey. In order for rewards to have the reinforcing power that they are designed to have, we must use reinforcers that are desired by the child. All too often parents and teachers try to make sugar pops and M & Ms work for every child, when not all children necessarily have a liking for either one of these. The problem is that parents are choosing reinforcers that they personally like or ones they believe the children will like, rather than allowing the children to have some input in the choice of reinforcers.

Parents would do well to administer a reinforcement survey (see Figure 10.1), a series of open-ended statements designed to pinpoint the types of reinforcers a child desires and responds to best.

Figure 10.1

Reinforcement Survey

1. My favorite adult is _____.
2. What I like to do with this person is _____.
3. The best reward anybody could give me is _____.
4. My favorite school subject is _____.
5. If I had some money ($5, $10, etc.), I would _____.
6. When I grow up, I want to be _____.
7. The person who likes me the most is _____.
8. Two things I like to do best are _____.
9. I feel terrific when _____.
10. The way I get money is _____.
11. When I have money, I like to _____.
12. Something I really want is _____.
13. I would please my teacher by _____.
14. The person I like most to give me rewards is _____.
15. The thing I like to do best in school is _____.
16. The activity I like to do best on weekends is _____.
17. If I did better in school, I wish my teacher would _____.
18. I would do my very best work if I knew I could get _____.
19. The place I would like to visit the most is _____.
20. When I am with my best friend, I like to _____.

Read the sentence stems to the child and have him provide his response in writing or tape record his responses (you may have the child give two or three answers in rank order).

Analyze the child's responses to determine whether he desires tactile-sensory, edible, tangible, token, activity, or social reinforcers. You may find that the child only likes one or two types of reinforcers. One home educating father of a gifted-LD boy administered this survey and found that Lego building blocks and GI Joe toys, both tangible reinforcers, were named the most. It would be wise to administer this reinforcement survey about once or twice per school month to see whether the child's desires are changing. Parents may wish to consult R. Hall and M. Hall[6] for additional guidelines on selecting reinforcers.

Once you have a list of potential reinforcers, you can then decide which good behaviors (e.g., attention span, remaining in seat, answering more math questions, etc.) need to be increased and, hence, reinforced. A good rule of thumb to follow is to concentrate on no more than one to three good behaviors at a time. Any more than three behaviors may be too much for a parent to keep up with.

After you decide which behaviors you need to reinforce, you must determine how much of the behavior the child must show you in a given time frame in order to receive the reinforcer. For example, you may have concluded that your son generally completes only 5 of 10 math problems successfully on a typical assignment. You decide initially that he will receive the reinforcer if he can complete at least 6 or 7 problems correctly. Over the course of several weeks, you can gradually increase the number of math problems you want the child to complete successfully in order to receive the reinforcer. Keep increasing the behavior goal gradually across several days or weeks until you reach the desired level of mastery (e.g., 90% to 100% correct math problems).

Positive reinforcement programs work best when parents set reasonable, attainable behavior goals and when the reinforcer is given liberally, immediately (avoid long delays), and frequently. It is also important that parents reinforce the desired behavior at *each* occurrence. Remember, our children are counting on us to be consistent in our promise of delivering the reward regularly and on time. Above all, the child should only receive the reinforcer *contingent* upon meeting the designated behavior goal (i.e., 8 of 10 math problems, remaining in seat for 5 minutes, etc.). To give the child the reward when he just gives his best effort or whenever you feel that he should get the reinforcer may result in you unintentionally reinforcing unacceptable behavior. Ensuring that the child cannot get a reinforcer at any other time of the day (e.g., computer time in the evening hours) will maximize its effect when using it during the home school program.

Token Systems. Giving tokens to a child for good behavior or work done well in school is much like an employer giving an employee pay for his work rendered on the job. One of great advantages of token systems is that the child can trade in his tokens for a variety of edible, tangible, and activity reinforcers, much like adults will use cash to purchase different items. Children will readily recognize the purchasing power of tokens in getting the specific reinforcers they desire the most, and they will work diligently and hard to get them.

Interestingly, the token in and of itself has no power. Tokens in a stored box, like cash in one's bank account, do little good in reinforcing appropriate behavior. Only when the tokens are exchanged for something desirable or useful do we see the powerful effect that tokens have on increasing appropriate behaviors in children. It is important that parents consider the following steps in developing and implementing effective token systems.

1. Select a token. Examples of tokens would include stickers, checkers, tickets, smiley faces, points on a card, hole punches on a card, and so on. Choosing the type of token is a critical first step and should be guided by a number of important principles. One, make sure it is *safe*. For example, if you are working with mentally disabled students, you would choose a token that couldn't be swallowed. Two, the token should be *fool-proof*. That is, the student should not be able to duplicate or counterfeit it on his own. Using common objects that can naturally be found around the home as tokens would not be wise, since the child could in a moment of deception issue himself additional tokens that he has not earned.

One classroom teacher reported that she cut one-inch square pieces of different colored construction paper to use as tokens. Although she cut and issued less than a hundred tokens to use for one week with her students, the total number of tokens had miraculously multiplied to several hundred a couple of days later when the students were ready to trade-in! Construction paper, which can easily be purchased just about anywhere, clearly was not a good choice for tokens.

Three, make the token *durable*. Some children will save their earned tokens for long periods of time. Paper tokens, therefore, would probably not be the most durable material. The same teacher described above who had the counterfeiting problem also had a problem with durability. The students in her class were middle school age, and the boys in particular would place their earned (and counterfeited!) tokens in their back pockets for safe keeping. Of course, after several days of perspiration, the construction paper tokens became quite moist, mangled, and discolored. Laminating the paper with plastic might have allowed the tokens to be more durable.

A fourth principle is that the token should be *inexpensive*. The bulk of money invested in a token system should not be in the token, rather in the back-up rewards and prizes that the student will be able to trade for the tokens. Finally, make sure that the token is *undesirable* to the student. This is important because one of the advantages of a token system is the ease with which the teacher can administer the token reinforcer for acceptable behavior right on the spot without interrupting on-going instruction.

One thrifty teacher reported that she chose old baseball cards she had purchased inexpensively at a yard sale as her token. Unfortunately, she realized on the first day of her token program that the baseball cards were a poor choice. The boys in the class, upon receiving the token (baseball cards) promptly for meeting their individual behavior goals, wanted to stop immediately and read the description of the athlete written on the backs of the cards. The baseball cards not only interrupted the teacher's lesson, but eventually caused a disruption.

2. Determine back-up reinforcers. Back-up reinforcers are the rewards for which the child will trade his earned tokens. These can be as varied as your imagination and pocketbook will allow. Be careful to choose reinforcers that are desired by the child. It would be best to administer the reinforcement survey (discussed earlier) to get ideas of the types of reinforcers the child would like to have. It will be important to choose several reinforcers that range in value from basic need items such as pencils, recess time, using a calculator, etc., to luxury items that may include toys and trinkets that the child has indicated that he would like to have. The pool of back-up reinforcers may cover the gamut of reinforcer types from edible, to tangible, to activity reinforcers.

3. Establish token-exchange prices. Setting trade-in prices is your decision alone, based on observations of your child and his needs. Keep these four economic principles in mind as you set your prices (see Figure 10.2 for an example of one home school mother's trade-in prices):

1. The number of tokens per reinforcer should initially be small to insure immediate success for the student. Present the child with only a few basic need and luxury items at first, and let the price of the basic need items be less than that of the luxury items.

2. As token-earning behaviors and earned tokens increase, gradually increase the cost of the back-up items and increase the variety of items from which the child may choose.

3. As the program progresses and the child's ability to earn tokens increases, bring in more luxury items (which will in effect cause the child to use up his earned tokens quicker so that he will not be tempted to save them for later to perhaps take a day off from home school).

4. In the final stages, increase token prices of basic need items and lower the prices for luxury items.

Figure 10.2

Token Trade-In Prices for an LD Boy

Food Rewards (5 to 25 pennies)

- penny candy
- jelly beans
- gummy bears
- lollipops
- marshmallows
- cookies
- kool-aid
- flavored ice cubes
- sodas
- ice cream
- restaurant meal

Activity Rewards (25 to 200 pennies)

- art project
- television programs
- craft project
- ride on 4-wheel motor bike
- shopping with mom
- baking cookies with mom
- swim at grandmother's
- fishing with dad
- sleep over with friend
- rent a video
- play a computer game
- trip to sports event or movies

Tangible Rewards (250 pennies)

- toy from store

---

4. Establish how and when tokens are exchanged. The back-up rewards and corresponding token prices should be posted in a very conspicuous place in the home. For those children who cannot read, use pictures instead of words on the token trade-in menu. Parents might consider designating one corner of a room as the "Token Trade-in Store." There should be frequent trade-in times in the initial stages of the program. Gradually train the child to be able to wait longer to receive reinforcement. We recommend the following schedule: (1) two or three trade-in times per hour for the first week; (2) several times per day for the second week; (3) once per day for the third week; (4) once every other day for the fourth week; and (5) once per week in the fifth week and beyond.

5. Define rules for acceptable behaviors or tasks. Choosing the token-earning behavior or skill in which your child needs to improve, like other aspects of the token program, will be your decision. You may want to keep several principles in mind:

1. Choose only behaviors which are observable (i.e., they can be seen) and measurable (i.e., they can be counted).
2. Tell your child the acceptable level of performance that you are looking for (e.g., remain in seat 90% of the time; complete 85% of math problems correctly).
3. Start with only a few token-earning behaviors, making sure you include some easy, attainable behaviors—you probably should not address more than three different behaviors at one time.
4. Make sure your child possesses the prerequisite skills he needs in order to perform the behavior acceptably before you begin (e.g., he must be able to simplify fractions before he can add fractions with unlike denominators).

6. Field-test before implementing. This can be done easily by observing the child over several school days and keeping a record of token points that he would be earning for certain behaviors if the program were in effect. This will allow you to see how many tokens he would be earning if this were a real situation. Be careful not to tell the student what you are doing. You should be able to use this experimental data to assess the prices for back-up reinforcers that you have set and make adjustments accordingly.

A number of final recommendations will make a token program successful. One, plan a time to teach your child what to expect from the token program and how it will operate. Give an example and model how the tokens will be delivered to him and how he will exchange his tokens for back-up rewards. Two, be careful to issue a social reinforcer (e.g., "Great job on your reading words!") along with tokens each time. Finally, keep careful records of tokens issued and redeemed, perhaps in your gradebook.

For more information on token programs, parents may want to secure one or both of the following recent publications available from the ADD Warehouse (see Appendix A): *Home Token Economy: An Incentive Program for Children and Their Parents*[7] and *Behavior Management At Home: A Token Economy Program for Children and Teens.*[8] Ayllon and McKittrick[9] have also produced a small booklet that provides additional guidelines for setting up token programs (available from Pro-Ed; see Appendix A for mailing address).

Behavior Contracts. Since contracts are a natural part of our everyday lives, parents may want to use this concept in managing behavior. Although some contractual agreements in real life are verbal in nature, contracts that are written tend to be more binding. So it should be with behavioral contracts that we implement in the home with children. They should be written.

It is probably best to negotiate[10] the details and specifics of the contract with the child, if he is of age to provide input about himself (i.e., middle school age or older). Contracts, like other behavior management techniques, must specify a behavior that needs to be improved and a reinforcer that can be earned contingent upon performing the behavior or skill at the required level of proficiency.

Behavioral contracts for younger, elementary-age children will look noticeably different from those for adolescents. Contracts for children will have more age-appropriate wording and should be embellished with color and graphics (see Figure 10.3). Contracts for older students, on the other hand, should be more legal and plainer in appearance (see Figure 10.4). Properly designed contracts should contain the following elements:

- specific task or behavior;
- degree of improvement or proficiency level;
- beginning time—day and time contract goes into effect;
- deadline for completion;
- reward the child will receive;
- teacher and student signatures (others, if desired);
- date under signature signifying signing of contract; and
- record of progress.

Figure 10.3

Elementary Behavior Contract

Going for the Finish Line!

If_____ can _____

_____

_____

for____days in a row beginning_____

and ending_____, then he will receive

_____.

—Signatures—

Student:_____ Date:_____

Mother:_____ Date:_____

Father: _____ Date:_____

—Check for Success—

☐ Day 1   ☐ Day 2   ☐ Day 3   ☐ Day 4   ☐ Day 5

Figure 10.4

Secondary Level Behavior Contract

✳ ✳ ✳ CONTRACTUAL AGREEMENT ✳ ✳ ✳

This contract represents an agreement between the Student and his Parents
All undersigned parties hereby pledge to fulfill the terms set out in this
contract. Attainment of these conditions, and by no other
means, qualifies the Student for the reward.

I,_____(Student) agree to_____

_____

_____

beginning_____, 19___ and ending_____, 19___.

If I fulfill the conditions of these terms, then_____ (Mother or Father)

agree to give me the following reward:_____

_____

_____.

AGREED AND ACCEPTED:

_____   _____
         Student   Mother or Father

Signed on this, the_____day of_____in the year of our Lord, 19___.

Record of progress:_____

_____

_____

Reduction Techniques

Since struggling learners will demonstrate both desirable and undesirable behaviors, it naturally follows that parents will need to develop and implement behavior management strategies that will address both goals of behavior change—increasing appropriate behaviors *and* decreasing inappropriate ones. Many parents and teachers prefer enhancement techniques like the ones described above since they emphasize the positive aspects of behavior change.

But what about times when children do too much of an unacceptable behavior, like pinching, hitting, or leaving an assigned area or task without permission? What does a parent do when preventative and short-term techniques have been exhausted and there is still no improvement? That's when we must employ *reduction* long-term behavior management techniques.

Reduction techniques are used to decrease the rate of or eradicate poor, undesirable, inappropriate behaviors. Reducing undesirable behaviors can be accomplished through positive reinforcement or punishment. We will discuss four reduction long-term techniques. One technique, differential reinforcement, makes use of positive reinforcement, and the other three—reprimands, time out, and overcorrection—are punishment procedures.

Differential Reinforcement. We have discussed using positive reinforcement as a means to increase good behaviors, but it can also be used to reduce unpleasant behaviors in a child. We call this technique *differential reinforcement*. One form has to do with reinforcing a child when he keeps a poor behavior at a designated low rate.

Consider a student who is having difficulty remembering to double-check his mathematics problems. The result is that he has a high rate of errors. His mother notes that, on each of the last three 20-problem assignments, he has missed 10, 12, and 8 problems. The parent decides to differentially reinforce the boy by giving him a reward only when he misses no more than 4 problems out of 20 (which would be an 80% success rate). This is called *differential reinforcement of low rate of response*. Of course, the success goal can be increased gradually over time by reducing the number of missed answers even more.

Another form of differential reinforcement deals with giving a child a reward only when he demonstrates a behavior that is the exact opposite of the target problem behavior. For example, suppose a child is out of his seat constantly during a 15-minute lesson. The mother instructs the child that he will receive a reward only if he remains in his seat the entire 15-minute lesson. In-seat behavior is totally incompatible with out-of-seat behavior, that is, they cannot happen at the same moment in time. In-seat behavior is, in fact, the exact opposite of out-of-seat behavior, and in-seat behavior can only occur when out-of-seat behavior is not occurring. This is called *differential reinforcement of incompatible behavior.*

Reprimands. Reprimands are the mildest, most common, non-controversial form of punishment that can be used to reduce inappropriate behaviors. A reprimand is any expression of disapproval directed toward a child that may include:

- verbal statements (e.g., Mother says, "Susan...please keep your mind on your school work.");
- gestures (e.g., shaking finger, snap of a finger); and
- facial expressions (e.g., scowling look, staring eyes).

Generally, any one of these forms of reprimand used alone is ineffective. Parents can increase the chance that a reprimand will be effective, by combining two or all three forms of reprimand at one time. For example, a mother might say with a scowling look, "Jason...please keep your mind on your school work," as she shakes her finger.

The manner in which the reprimand is delivered is also important. It should be given during *low intensity* of behavior. By delivering the reprimand immediately when the behavior occurs, and when the child's behavior is only mildly disruptive rather than extremely disruptive, low intensity can be insured. The teacher should also deliver the reprimand in *close proximity* to the child. Distance between teacher and child only weakens the reprimand and increases the chance that the reprimand may be misdirected. A final critical element of an effective reprimand is *contact*, with can be done physically (e.g., a slight touch on the shoulder) or visually (e.g., eye contact). Parents may wish to secure a small booklet by Van Houten[11] that provides additional guidelines on delivering reprimands (available from Pro-Ed; see Appendix A).

Parents should not avoid using punishment techniques. While it may be painful for both the parent and the child, punishment is a necessary and Biblically sound behavior management technique. Numerous Scripture passages support the use of punishment including Proverbs 13:24, Proverbs 19:18, Proverbs 22:15, Proverbs 23:14-15, and Proverbs 29:15.

Time Out. Time out is a more intensive form of punishment. Time out occurs when a student is denied positive reinforcement (rewards) for a brief, specified period of time, not to exceed about 10 minutes. Initially, time out should range from one to two minutes. As additional time out periods become necessary, the amount of time the child is in time out can be increased.

There are three simple forms of time out: (1) contingency observation time out; (2) isolation time out; and (3) seclusion time out. The types of time out, when used in this order over separate behavior infractions, grow increasingly more punishing. For example, seclusion time denies the child more reinforcing opportunities than isolation time out, and isolation time out more than contingency observation time out. Parents should begin with contingency observation time out and gradually move toward the other two types, if the behavior worsens or persists. Each form of time out is described below:

1. **Contingency observation time out**—the child is allowed to *see* and *hear* other brothers and sisters succeeding and receiving rewards while he continues with his school work and remains with the group, but he is not allowed to receive rewards (e.g., Johnny is allowed to remain in the home school room, perhaps even at the same table where everyone else is; however, he cannot receive rewards. He may also be asked to back his chair away from the table for the time out period.)

2. **Isolation time out**—the child is denied the privilege of receiving rewards, and he is not allowed to see other brothers and sisters getting rewards either, although he may be allowed to *hear* what is going on (e.g., Johnny is placed in the corner of the home school room, perhaps at a small table with a portable study carrel surrounding him, and he sits or works alone.)

3. **Seclusion time out**—the child is removed completely from the learning environment, not able to receive rewards, nor is he permitted to see, hear, or be in the presence of others who are involved in reward-earning activities (e.g., Johnny is asked to go sit in another room in the home, completely separate from mother, brothers, and sisters.).

Giving careful attention to several considerations will make time out more effective. One, make sure that sending the child to time out does not allow him an opportunity to avoid or escape an unpleasant task. For example, a student may be uncooperative because he does not want to complete a challenging academic task. Sending him to time out only to allow him to return sometime later and do some other school task that may be easier would be allowing him to avoid something unpleasant. Time out in this case would prove to be counterproductive. The parent should make it clear to the child that, upon returning to the learning situation, he will still have to complete the task that he was attempting to avoid by misbehaving prior to being sent to time out.

Two, do not administer time out as a substitute for a more aversive punishment that has been promised. This would occur when a parent has warned a child that he may have to do three hours of yard work if he does not correct his behavior, and then the parent capitulates and sends the child to time out instead. Finally, make sure that the environment of the time out setting is not more reinforcing that the reward-earning, time-in learning environment. Sending a child to the family room (which may have a television, stereo, video games, card games, etc.) for seclusion time out in effect provides him with a more reinforcing environment. We refer parents to R. Hall and M. Hall[12] for additional information on time out procedures.

Overcorrection. Overcorrection is the most recently developed form of punishment. Although typically used in institutional settings for individuals who aggressively destroy or deface property, it can be generalized nicely to home settings. Interestingly, there is a Scriptural basis for overcorrection. In Leviticus 6:2-7, we read instructions given to Moses by God concerning how he was to discipline those under his leadership who have sinned. The passage reads:

If a soul sin, and commit a trespass against the Lord, and lie unto his neighbor in that which was delivered him to keep, or in fellowship, or in a thing taken away by violence, or hath deceived his neighbor; Or have found that which was lost, and lieth concerning it, and sweareth falsely; in any of all these that a man doeth, sinning therein; Then it shall be, because he hath sinned, and is guilty, that he shall restore that which he took violently away, or the thing which he had deceitfully gotten, or that which was delivered him to keep, or the lost thing which he found, Or all that about which he hath sworn falsely; he shall even restore it in the principal, and shall add the fifth part more thereto, and give it unto him to whom it appertaineth...

Simply put, God intended for a person who had committed a trespass to restore what was damaged or taken to its original state. But in addition to this, God instructed that the offender was to go beyond restoration of the principal amount and do a fifth more (i.e., add 20% to the original amount).

Restitution. The *restore-plus* principle found in the book of Leviticus is evident in the *restitutional* form of overcorrection used by some special educators today. Consider an angry student, who enters the classroom and intentionally knocks over a stack of books on the teacher's desk. Restitutional overcorrection occurs when the teacher immediately instructs the student to place the books back on the desk in a stack as they originally were when he entered. In addition, the teacher has the student perform an extra chore (i.e., overcorrecting for the inappropriate behavior) such as cleaning the erasure marks in all of the books, or perhaps cleaning and straightening all of the books on the book shelf in the classroom. A resource by Azrin and Besalel[13] that provides more information on how to use overcorrection is available from Pro-Ed (see Appendix A).

Positive Practice. Sometimes viewed as another form of overcorrection, positive practice requires the student to perform a positive behavior correctly in a repeated manner. For example, consider a parent who has been helping her child master multiplication facts. However, several of the nine-family multiplication facts continue to stump the child in multiplication problems. Having the child repeatedly write and say the specific nine facts that he has not mastered (perhaps 30 times in succession) each time the error occurs in isolation or in a math problem would provide him with the needed positive practice that may improve his mastery. Parents can learn more about the use of positive practice by referring to Azrin and Besalel.[14]

Maintain a Balance

While effective teachers manage their classroom and educational programs, they do not *manage* a child's behavior per se. It is the same with parents in the home. In reality, what parents are managing are the environmental factors and variables in the home that directly affect and impact their child's behavior. More important, behavior management techniques influence a child's will to behave more appropriately.

Parents must implement the full range of behavior management techniques to address both appropriate and inappropriate behavior in their struggling learners. The temptation, however, will be to employ only the reward-type enhancement techniques and avoid the reduction techniques altogether, particularly the punishment-type techniques. We believe the best approach is to maintain a balance between the two. Using only positive reinforcement may unintentionally cause a child to think that he has no inappropriate behaviors that need fixing. On the other hand, an inordinate emphasis on punishment may depress a child and lead him to think that he can do nothing right.

If we are truly concerned about educating the whole child, we must implement both positive reinforcement and punishment techniques as the need arises. It is simply the right thing to do, for this is the pattern of God our Father in Scripture. We concur with Dr. Saul Axelrod, who maintains:

> The preference that teachers have for reinforcement techniques over punishment is understandable and commendable. The conflict is that punishment procedures often work where reinforcement techniques do not. The failure to use punishment under these conditions can be contrary to a student's long-term best interests....It should...be understood that punishment is as natural a learning process as reinforcement.[15]

[1]Nelson (1981)
[2]W. Camp & B. Camp (1989)
[3]O'Leary & Schneider (1987)
[4]R. Hall & M. Hall (1980b)
[5]Axelrod (1983)
[6]R. Hall & M. Hall (1980a)
[7]Alvord (1973)
[8]Parker (1995)
[9]Ayllon & McKittrick (1982)
[10]R. Hall & M. Hall (1982)
[11]Van Houten (1980)
[12]R. Hall & M. Hall (1980c)
[13]Azrin & Besalel (1980)
[14]Azrin & Besalel (1981)
[15]Axelrod (1983)

Resources and Suppliers

A to Z Guide to Your Child's Behavior
David Mrazek, M.D. & William
Garrison, Ph.D. with Laura Elliot
ADD Warehouse
No. 6302 $15

Academic Therapy Publications*
20 Commercial Blvd.
Novato, CA   94949-6191
(800) 422-7249

*ADAPT: Attention Deficit Accommo-
dation Plan for Teaching*
Harvey C. Parker, Ph D
ADD Warehouse
No. 0900A $20

ADD Warehouse*
300 Northwest 70th Ave., Suite 102
Plantation, FL   3317
(800) ADD-WARE

*The ADD Hyperactivity Workbook
for Parents, Teachers, and Kids*
Harvey C. Parker, Ph.D
ADD Warehouse
No. 0954 $14

American Guidance Service*
P.O. Box 99
Circle Pines, MN   55014-1796
(800) 328-2560

Audio Memory
501 Cliff Dr.
Newport Beach, CA   92663
(800) 365-SING

AWANA Bible Memory
Program for disabled students
1 E. Bode Rd.
Streamwood, IL   60107
(708) 213-2000

Bob Jones University Press*
Greenville, SC 29614
800-845-5731
e-mail: lgrover@wpo.bju.edu

CA Career Aids*
20417 Nordhoff St. Dept. P4
Chatsworth, CA   91311
(818) 341-9134

Chaselle, Inc.*
P.O. Box 2097
9645 Gerwig Lane
Columbia, MD   21046
(800) 628-8608

Continental Press*
520 E. Bainbridge St.
Elizabethtown, PA   17022
(800) 233-0659

Council for Exceptional Children*
1920 Association Dr.
Dept K10921
Reston, VA   22091-1589
(703) 620-3660

Creative Publications*
5040 West 111th St.
Oak Lawn, IL   60453
(800) 624-0822

*Brochure available

Curriculum Associates*
5 Esquire Rd.
North Billerica, MA   01862-9987
(800) 225-0248

DLM*
P.O. Box 4000
One DLM Park
Allen, TX   75002
(800) 527-4747

Edmark Corporation*
P.O. Box 3903
Bellevue, WA   98009-3903
(800) 426-0856

Education PLUS® *
Dr. Ron & Inge Cannon
P.O. Box 1350
Taylors, SC 29687
(864) 609-5411
Fax: (864) 609-5678
Internet: www.edplus.com

Exceptional Diagnostics*
Joe P. Sutton, Ph.D.
Certified Educational Diagnostician
220 Douglas Dr.
Simpsonville, SC   29681
Tel./Fax: (864) 967-4729
e-mail: suttonjp@juno.com

Goal Card Program
Harvey C. Parker, Ph.D.
ADD Warehouse
No. 0953 $15

*Hands-On Equations® *
Borenson and Associates
P.O. Box 3328
Allentown, PA   18106
(610) 820-5575

Happy Time Course
Bible curriculum for disabled students
Scripture Press Publications
1825 College Ave.
Wheaton, IL   60187
(800) 323-9409

Hawthorne*
800 Gray Oak Dr.
Columbia, MO   65201
(800) 542-1673

Helping Your Hyperactive Child
John F. Taylor, Ph.D.
Add Warehouse
No. 3010 $20

✻ High Noon Books*
High interest/low vocabulary books
20 Commercial Blvd.
Novato, CA   94949-6191
(800) 422-7249

Homeschooling Today Magazine
Debbie Strayer, Editor
P.O. Box 1425
Melrose, FL   32666
(904) 475-3088
e-mail: hstodaymag@aol.com

Home Run Enterprises
Mike and Cathy Duffy
16172 Huxley Circle
Westminster, CA   92683
(714) 841-1220
Fax: (714) 841-5584

Home School Legal Defense Association
P.O. Box 159
Paeonian Springs, VA   22129
(703) 338-5600

*Brochure available

Home Token Economy
Jack R. Alvord, Ph.D.
ADD Warehouse
No. 1975 $11

Independent Strategies for Efficient Study
Karen Rooney, Ph.D.
ADD Warehouse
No. 3501 $28

Lakeshore Learning Materials*
2695 E. Dominquez St.
P.O. Box 6261
Carson, CA 90749
(800) 421-5354

Library of Special Education*
A Newbridge Book Club
3000 Cindel Dr.
Delran, NJ 08370-0001
(609) 786-9778

LinguiSystems*
3100 4th Ave.
P.O. Box 747
East Moline, IL 61244
(800) 755-2377

Listen, Look, and Think: A Self-regulation Program for Children
Harvey C. Parker, Ph.D.
ADD Warehouse
No. 0955 $20

Midwest Publications*
P.O. Box 448
Pacific Grove, CA 93950
(800) 458-4849

MotivAider
Steve Levinson, Ph.D.
ADD Warehouse
No. 4101 $90

National Challenged Homeschoolers Associated Network (NATHHAN)
Tom & Sherry Bushnell, Founders
5383 Alpine Rd. SE
Olalla, WA 98359
(206) 857-4257
e-mail: nathanews@aol.com

The Notebook Organizer
ADD Warehouse
No. 0962 $16

Parents Are Teachers
Wesley C. Becker, Ph.D.
ADD Warehouse
No. 1974 $16

A Parent's Guide: Attention Deficit Hyperactivity Disorder in Children
Sam Goldstein, Ph.D. and Michael Goldstein, Ph.D.
ADD Warehouse
No. 1566 $28 (10/pkg.)

The Parents' Hyperactivity Handbook: Helping the Fidgety Child
David M. Paltin, Ph.D.
ADD Warehouse
No. 1770 $28

Pro-Ed*
8700 Shoal Creek Blvd.
Austin, TX 78757-6897
(512) 451-3246

Recordings for the Blind*
20 Roszel Rd.
Princeton, NJ 08540
(800) 221-4792

Shepherds Curriculum
Bible instruction for disabled students
Shepherds, Inc.
Box 400
Union Grove, WI 53182
(414) 878-5620

*Brochure available

Sing 'n Learn
2626 Club Meadow
Garland, TX   75043
(214) 278-1973

Special Education: A Biblical Approach
Joe P. Sutton, Ph.D., Editor
Hidden Treasure Publications
18 Hammet St.
Greenville, SC   29609
(864) 235-6848 $19.95

*Special Times**
Computer Software Reviews
Cambridge Development Laboratory, Inc.
86 West St.
Waltham, MA   02154
(800) 637-0047
(617) 890-4640 in Massachusetts

Teachables*
Gayle M. Wylie, MS, CCC/SLP
Licensed Speech-Language Pathologist and Home Educating Consultant
Rt. 2 Box 210
Harrisonburg, VA   22801
(540) 433-8522

Thinking Publications*
Division of McKinley Companies, Inc.
1731 Westgate Rd.
P.O. Box 163
Eau Claire, WI   54702-0163
(800) 255-GROW

*Touch Math**
Innovative Learning Concepts, Inc.
6760 Corporate Dr.
Colorado Springs, CO   80919-1999
(800) 888-9191

Why Won't My Child Pay Attention
Sam Goldstein, Ph.D.   (video)
Michael Goldstein, M.D.
ADD Warehouse
No. 1562 $30

Wise Choice Educational Services*
Assessment and Consultation
Suzanne Day, M.A.
Psychoeducational Consultant
506 Ferndale Dr., North
Barrie, Ontario, CANADA
L4M 4S4
(705) 726-5971

Your Hyperactive Child: A Parent's Guide to Coping with ADD
Barbara Ingersoll, Ph.D.
ADD Warehouse
No. 0434 $10

*Brochure available

References

Alvord, J. R. (1973). *Home token economy: An incentive program for children and their parents.* Champaign, IL: Research Press.

American Heritage Dictionary (2nd College Ed.). (1985). Boston, MA: Houghton Mifflin.

American Psychiatric Association. (1994). *Diagnostic and statistical manual of mental disorder* (DSM-IV, 4th ed.). Washington, DC: Author.

Armstrong, D. G., Henson, K. T., & Savage, T. V. (1993). *Education: An introduction* (4th ed.). New York: Macmillan.

Audio Memory. (1996). [Product postcard advertisement]. Newport Beach, CA: Author.

Axelrod, S. (1983). *Behavior management for the classroom teacher.* New York: McGraw-Hill.

Ayllon, T., & McKittrick, S. M. (1982). *How to set up a token economy.* Austin, TX: Pro-Ed.

Azrin, N. H., & Besalel, V. A. (1980). *How to use overcorrection.* Austin, TX: Pro-Ed.

Azrin, N. H., & Besalel, V. A. (1981). *How to use positive practice.* Austin, TX: Pro-Ed.

Barkley, R. A. (1996, November 8). *Attention deficit hyperactivity disorder in children and adults.* Professional development workshop sponsored by the Distinctive Educational Center and the Learning Disability Association of S.C., Cayce, SC.

Becker, W. C., Engelmann, S., & Thomas, D. R. (1975). *Teaching II: Cognitive learning and instruction.* Chicago, IL: Science Research Associates.

Beery, K. E. (1997). *The Developmental Test of Visual-Motor Integration* (4th ed.). Cleveland, OH: Modern Curriculum Press.

Beechick, R. (1992). Hope for dyslexics. *Homeschooling Today, 1*(2), 45-49.

Behymer, M. E. (1993). *Trainable and severely/profoundly mentally retarded students.* In J. P. Sutton (Ed.), Special education: A Biblical approach (pp. 287-330). Greenville, SC: Hidden Treasure Publications.

Bender, L. A. (1938). *Visual Motor Gestalt Test*. New York: American Orthopsychiatric Association.

Bley, N. S., & Thornton, C. A. (1995). *Teaching mathematics to students with learning disabilities* (3rd ed.). Austin, TX: Pro-Ed.

Bliss, E. C. (1983). *Doing it now*. New York, NY: Scribner.

Borenson, H. (1994). *The Hands-On Equations Learning System*. Allentown, PA: Borenson and Associates.

Bragstad, B. J., & Stumpf, S. M. (1987). *A guidebook for teaching study skills and motivation*. Needham Heights, MA: Allyn & Bacon.

Brigance, A. H. (1983). *BRIGANCE Diagnostic Comprehensive Inventory of Basic Skills*. North Billerica, MA: Curriculum Associates.

Brill, R. G., MacNeil, B., & Newman, L. R. (1986). Framework for appropriate programs for deaf children. *American Annals of the Deaf, 131*(2), 65-77.

Brown, V. L., Hammill, D. D., & Wiederholt, L. (1986). *Test of Reading Comprehension: Revised Edition*. Austin, TX: Pro-Ed.

Brown, V., & McEntire, E. (1984). *Test of Mathematical Abilities*. Austin, TX: Pro-Ed.

Bullock, J. (1992). New Products: *Touch Math* (4th ed.). *Intervention in School and Clinic, 28*, 119-122.

Bullock, J. (1994). *Touch Math* (4th ed.). Colorado Springs, CO: Innovative Learning Concepts.

Bursuck, W. D., Rose, E., Cowen, S., & Yahaya, M. A. (1989). Nationwide survey of postsecondary education services for students with learning disabilities. *Exceptional Children, 56*, 236-245.

Cambridge Development Laboratory, Inc. (1995, Spring). *Special times: Special education software for grades K-12* [catalog]. Waltham, MA: Author.

Camp, W., & Camp, B. (1989). [Workshop on behavior management techniques]. Charlottesville, VA.

Cannon, R. J., & Cannon, I. P. (1996). *Education PLUS® Patterning Learning Upon Scripture curriculum sampler*. Mauldin, SC: Education PLUS®.

Carbo, M. (1996). Whole language or phonics? Use both! *Education, 117*, 60-63.

Carman, R. A., & Adams, W. R. (1972). *Study skills: A student's guide for survival*. New York: Wiley.

Clements, S. D. (1966). *Minimal brain dysfunction in children: Terminology and identification.* NINDB Monograph No. 3 Washington, DC: U.S. Department of Health, Education and Welfare.

Cohen, S. B. (1993). Effective instruction: Principles and strategies for programs. In B. S. Billingsley (Ed.), *Program leadership for serving students with disabilities* (pp. 169-252). Richmond, VA: Virginia Department of Education.

Colangelo, N., & Davis, G. A. (1991). Introduction and historical overview. In N. Colangelo & G. A. Davis (Eds.), *Handbook of gifted education* (pp. 3-13), Needham Heights, MA: Allyn & Bacon.

Connolly, A. J. (1988). *Keymath-Revised: A Diagnostic Inventory of Essential Mathematics.* Circle Pines, MN: American Guidance Service.

Council for Exceptional Children. (1994). Classroom tips for ADD. *CEC Today, 1*(2), 11.

Cronin, M. E., & Currie, P. S. (1984). Study skills: A resource guide for practitioners. *Remedial and Special Education, 5*(2), 61-69.

Duffy, M., & Duffy, C. (1997). *Christian home educators' curriculum manual. Elementary grades.* Westminster, CA: Grove Publishing.

Dunlap, J. M. (1994). Additional suggestions [Teaching children with special needs]. *The Teaching Home, 12*(4), 45.

Durrell, D., & Catterson, J. (1980). *Durrell Analysis of Reading Difficulty.* San Antonio, TX: Psychological Corporation.

DuPaul, G. J., Anastopoulos, A.D., Power, T.J., Murphy, K.R., & Barkley, R.A. (1996, November 8). *ADHD Rating Scale-IV.* Draft of instrument disseminated by R.A. Barkley at professional development seminar, Cayse, SC.

Duvall, S. (1994, October). *The effects of home education on children with learning disabilities.* Paper presented at the National Christian Home Education Leadership Conference, Phoenix, AZ.

Ellis, E. S., & Lenz, B. K. (1987). A component analysis of effective learning strategies for LD students. *Learning Disabilities Focus, 2*(2), 94-107.

Engelmann, S. E., & Bruner, E. C. (1988). *Reading mastery: DISTAR reading.* Chicago, IL: Science Research Associates.

Engelmann, S. E., & Carnine, D. (1972). *DISTAR Arithmetic III.* Chicago, IL: Science Research Associates.

Engelmann, S. E., & Carnine, D. (1975). *DISTAR Arithmetic I.* Chicago, IL: Science Research Associates.

Engelmann, S. E., & Carnine, D. (1976). *DISTAR Arithmetic II*. Chicago, IL: Science Research Associates.

Englert, C. S. (1983). Measuring special education teacher effectiveness. *Exceptional Children, 50*, 247-254.

Englert, C. S. (1984). Measuring teacher effectiveness from the teacher's point of view. *Focus on Exceptional Children, 17*, 1-15.

Englert, C. S., & Thomas, C. C. (1982). Management of task involvement in special education classrooms: Implications for teacher preparation. *Teacher Education and Special Education, 5*, 3-10.

Federal Register. (1977). *Procedures for evaluating specific learning disabilities*. Washington, DC: Department of Health, Education, and Welfare, December 29.

Fernald, G. (1943). *Remedial techniques in basic school subjects*. New York: McGraw-Hill.

Fernald, G. (1988). *Remedial techniques in basic school subjects*. Austin, TX: Pro-Ed.

Fichter, R. (1993). Learning disabilities. In J. P. Sutton (Ed.), *Special education: A Biblical approach* (pp. 211-252). Greenville, SC: Hidden Treasures Publications.

Flynn, G. (1994). Setting goals and reporting progress. *The Teaching Home, 12*(4), 43.

Fouse, B., & Brians, S. (1993). *A primer on attention deficit disorder*. Bloomington, IN: Phi Delta Kappa Educational Foundation.

Frankenburg, W., Dodds, J., Archer, P., Bresnick, B., Maschaa, P, Edelman, N., & Shapiro, H. (1990). *Denver II Screening. Denver, CO:* Denver Developmental Materials, Inc.

Fulk, B. M., & Stormont-Spurgin, M. (1995). Fourteen spelling strategies for students with learning disabilities. *Intervention in School and Clinic, 31*(1), 16-20.

Gardner, M. F. (1985). *Test of Auditory-Perceptual Skills*. Burlingame, CA: Psychological and Educational Publications.

Garnett, K. (1991). Meeting the needs of children with ADD. *DLD Times, 8*(2), 4.

Gessell, J. K. (1983). *Diagnostic Mathematics Inventory/Mathematics System*. Monterey, CA: CTB/McGraw-Hill.

Giordano, G. (1984). *Teaching writing to LD students*. Rockville, MD: Aspen.

Gfeller, K. E. (1986). Musical mnemonics for learning disabled children. *Teaching Exceptional Children, 19*, 28-30.

Goldstein, S. (Speaker). (1989). *Why won't my child pay attention?* (Video). Salt Lake City, UT: Neurology, Learning and Behavior Center.

Good, T. L. (1979). Teacher effectiveness in the elementary school. *Journal of Teacher Education, 30*, 52-64.

Gordon, J., Vaughn, S., & Schumm, J. S. (1993). Spelling interventions: A review of literature and implications for instruction for students with learning disabilities. *Learning Disabilities Research and Practice, 8*, 175-181.

Graham, S., & Freeman, S. (1985). Strategy training and teacher- vs. student-controlled conditions: Effects on LD students' spelling performance. *Learning Disability Quarterly, 8*, 267-274.

Greenbaum, C. R. (1987). *Spellmaster Assessment and Teaching System*. Austin, TX: Pro-Ed.

Haffner, M. A., & Ireland, S. (1990, January). Operation N.O.U.N. *The Mailbox, 11*(6), 17.

Hall, R. V., & Hall, M. C. (1980a). *How to select reinforcers*. Austin, TX: Pro-Ed.

Hall, R. V., & Hall, M. C. (1980b) *How to use planned ignoring (extinction)*. Austin, TX: Pro-Ed.

Hall, R. V., & Hall, M. C. (1980c). *How to use time out*. Austin, TX: Pro-Ed.

Hall, R. V., & Hall, M. C. (1982). *How to negotiate a behavioral contract*. Austin, TX: Pro-Ed.

Hallahan, D. P., Hall, R. J., Ianna, S. O., Kneedler, R. D., Lloyd, J. W., Loper, A. B., & Reeve, R. E. (1983). Summary of research findings at the University of Virginia Learning Disabilities Research Institute. *Exceptional Educational Quarterly, 4*, 95-114.

Hallahan, D. P., & Kauffman, J. M. (1991). *Exceptional children: Introduction to special education* (5th ed.). Englewood Cliffs, NJ: Prentice Hall.

Hammill, D., & Larsen, S. (1988). *Test of Written Language*. Austin, TX: Pro-Ed.

Hammill, D. D. (1991). *Detroit Test of Learning Aptitude-3rd Edition*. Austin, TX: Pro-Ed.

Haynes, M. C., & Jenkins, J. R. (1986). Reading instruction. *American Educational Research Journal, 23*, 161-190.

Heckelman, R. G. (1969). The neurological impress method of remedial reading instruction. *Academic Therapy*, 4, 277-282.

Heuchert, C. M., & Long, N. (1980). A brief history of life space interviewing. *Pointer*, 25, 5-8.

Home School Legal Defense Association. (no date). *HSLDA's policy on home schooling children with special needs*. Paeonian Springs, VA: Author.

Home School Legal Defense Association. (1990). *A nationwide study of home education*. Paeonian Springs, VA: Author.

Houck, C. S., & McKenzie, R. G. (1988). *Paraprofessionals: Training for the classroom*. Circle Pines, MN: American Guidance Service.

Jones, B. (no date). *Chapel sayings of Dr. Bob Jones, Sr.* Greenville, SC: Bob Jones University Press.

Karlsen, B., & Gardner, E. (1985). *Stanford Diagnostic Reading Test* (3rd ed.). San Antonio, TX: The Psychological Corporation.

Kaufman, M., Agard, J. A., & Semmel, M. I. (1985). Methodology. In M. Kaufman, J. A. Agard, & M. I. Semmel (Eds.), *Mainstreaming: Learners and their environment* (pp. 21-53). Cambridge, MA: Brookline.

Kaufman, A., & Kaufman, N. (1983). *Kaufman Assessment Battery for Children*. Circle Pines, MN: American Guidance Service.

Kauffman, J. M. (1989). *Characteristics of behavior disorders of children and youth* (4th ed.). Columbus, OH: Merrill.

Kavale, K. A., & Forness, S. R. (1987). Substance over style: Assessing the efficacy of modality testing and teaching. *Exceptional Children, 54,* 228-239.

Keller, C. E., & Sutton, J. P. (1991). Specific mathematics disorders. In J. E. Obrzut & G. W. Hynd (Eds.), *Neuropsychological foundations in learning disabilities: A handbook of issues, methods and practice* (pp. 549-571). Orlando, FL: Academic Press.

Kelly, L. J., & Vergason, G. A. (1991). *Dictionary of special education and rehabilitation* (3rd ed.). Denver, CO: Love Publishing Co.

Lambert, N., Nihira, K., & Leland, H. (1993). *AAMR Adaptive Behavior Scale-School Second Edition-Examiner's manual*. Austin, TX: Pro-Ed.

Lapish, M. (1994). Parent-directed therapy at home. *The Teaching Home,* 12(4), 42.

Larsen, S., & Hammill, D. (1989). *Test of Legible Handwriting*. Austin, TX: Pro-Ed.

Larsen, S., & Hammill, D. (1986). *Test of Written Spelling-2*. Austin, TX: Pro-Ed.

Leinhardt, G., Zigmond, N., & Cooley, W. W. (1981). Reading instruction and its effects. *American Educational Research Journal, 18,* 343-361.

Lerner, J. W. (1989). *Learning disabilities: Theories, diagnosis, and teaching strategies* (5th ed.). Boston, MA: Houghton Mifflin.

Lerner, J. W., Lowenthal, B., & Lerner, S. R. (1995). *Attention deficit disorders: Assessment and teaching*. Pacific Grove, CA: Books/Cole.

Levey, E. (1984). *Methods and materials for LD I*. Lecture notes from graduate course taught at East Carolina University, Greenville, NC.

Luckasson, R., Coulter, D. L., Polloway, E. A., Reiss, S., Schalock, R. L., Snell, M. E., Spitalnick, D. M., & Stark, J. A. (1992). *Mental retardation:Diagnosis, classification, and systems of support* (9th ed.). Washington, DC: American Association on Mental Retardation.

Luftig, R. L. (1987). *Teaching the mentally retarded student: Curriculum, methods, and strategies*. Boston, MA: Allyn & Bacon.

Marland, S. P. (1972). *Education of the gifted and talented: Report to the Congress of the United States by the U.S. Commissioner of Education*. Washington, DC: Department of Health, Education, and Welfare.

Markwardt, F. (1989). *Peabody Individual Achievement Test-Revised*. CirclePines, MN: American Guidance Service.

McCarney, S. B. (1989). *Attention Deficit Disorder Evaluation Scale-Home/School Versions*. Columbia, MO: Hawthorne Educational Services.

McCarney, S. B. (1987). *Gifted Evaluation Scale*. Columbia, MO: Hawthorne Educational Services.

Melbar, G. (1990). Prayer and research allow mother to relax. *The Teaching Home, 8*(3), 54.

Mercer, C. D., & Mercer, A. R. (1989). *Teaching students with learning problems* (3rd ed.). Columbus, OH: Merrill.

Mercer, C. D., & Mercer, A. R. (1993). *Teaching students with learning problems* (4th ed.). Columbus, OH: Merrill.

Mills, D. (1995). I.E.P.'s made easy. *NATHHAN News, 3*(3), 20.

Nelson, C. M. (1981). Classroom management. In J. M. Kauffman & D. P. Hallahan (Eds.), *Handbook of special education* (pp. 663-667). Englewood Cliffs, NJ: Prentice-Hall.

Nelson, R., & Lingnugaris-Kraft, B. (1989). Postsecondary education for students with learning disabilities. *Exceptional Children, 56,* 246-265.

Nowacek, E. J., McKinney, J. D., & Hallahan, D. P. (1990). Instructional behaviors of more and less effective beginning regular and special educators. *Exceptional Children, 57*(2), 140-149.

O'Leary, K. D., & Schneider, M. R. (1987). *Catch'em being good: Approaches to motivation and discipline* [video]. Englewood Cliffs, NJ: Prentice Hall.

Parker, H. C. (1992). ADAPT: *Accommodations help students with attention deficit disorder.* Plantation, FL: ADD Warehouse.

Parker, H. C. (1995). *Behavior management at home: A token economy program for children and teens.* Plantation, Fl: ADD Warehouse.

Parker, H. C. (1990). *Listen, look, and think: A self-regulation program for children.* Plantation, FL: ADD Warehouse.

Parrish, S. (1995). Homeschooling the special needs child. *Homeschooling Today, 4*(2), 42-46.

Patton, J. R., Beirne-Smith, M., & Payne, J. S. (1990). *Mental retardation* (3rd ed.). Columbus, OH: Merrill.

Price, G. E., Dunn, R., & Dunn, K. (1985). *Learning Style Inventory* (LSI)/ *Productivity Environmental Preference Survey* (PEPS): Interpretive booklet. Lawrence, KS: Price Systems.

Psychological Corporation. (1992a). *Stanford Achievement Test* (8th ed.). San Antonio, TX: Harcourt Brace Jovanovich.

Psychological Corporation. (1992b). *Wechsler Individual Achievement Test.* San Antonio, TX: Harcourt Brace Jovanovich.

Psychological Corporation. (1991). *Wechsler Intelligence Scale for Children-Third Edition.* San Antonio, TX: Harcourt Brace Jovanovich.

Quay, H. C., & Peterson, D. R. (1983). *Revised Behavior Problem Checklist.* Longboat Key, FL: Author.

Reger, R. (1973). What is a resource room program? *Journal for Learning Disabilities, 6*(10), 609-614.

Reisman, F. K., & Kauffman, S. H. (1981). *Teaching mathematics to children with special needs.* Columbus, OH: Merrill.

Renzulli, J. S., & Reis, S. M. (1991). The School Enrichment Model: A comprehensive plan for the development of creative productivity. In N. Colangelo & G. A. Davis (Eds.), *Handbook of gifted education* (pp. 111-141). Needham Heights, MA: Allyn & Bacon.

Renzulli, J. S., Reis, S. M., & Smith, L. H. (1981). *The revolving door identification model.* Mansfield Center, CT: Creative Learning Press.

Richman, H, & Richman, S. (1993). *Guide to PA homeschool law* (5th ed.). Kittanning, PA: Pennsylvania Homeschoolers.

Robinson, S. (1987). Self-management: A tool for independence—A means of motivation. *LD Forum, 12*, 11-13.

Ruais, R. W. (1978). A low-stress algorithm for fractions. *Mathematics Teacher, 71*, 258-260.

Salvia, J., & Ysseldyke, J. E. (1995). *Assessment* (6th ed.). Boston, MA: Houghton Mifflin.

Scott, K. (1993). Multisensory mathematics for children with mild disabilities. *Exceptionality, 4*, 91-111.

Secord, W. (1981). *Test of Minimal Articulation Competence.* San Antonio, TX: Psychological Corporation.

Semel, E., Wiig, E., & Secord, W. (1989). *Clinical Evaluation of Language Function-Revised.* San Antonio, TX: Psychological Corporation.

Short, C. (1994). Teaching children with special needs. *The Teaching Home, 12*(4), 39-50.

Sindelar, P. T., Smith, M. A., Harriman, N. E., Hale, R. L., & Wilson, R. J. (1986). Teacher effectiveness in special education programs. *The Journal of Special Education, 20*, 195-207.

Sing 'n Spell. (1996). [Product postcard advertisement]. Garland, TX: Author.

Somerville, S. (1994). Special education and the law. *The Homeschool ADDvisor, 1*(1), 1-2.

Spain, T. (Producer). (1986). *To be a teacher* [News Special]. New York, NY: National Broadcasting Company.

Stephens, T. M. (1977). *Teaching skills to children with learning and beahvior disorders.* New York: Merrill/MacMillan.

Strayer, D. (1994). What's our position on learning problems. *Homeschooling Today, 3*(5), 1.

Sullivan, P. M. (1982). Adminisration modifications on the WISC-R Performance Scale with different categories of deaf children. *American Annals of the Deaf, 122*, 62-69.

Sutton, J. P. (1995). Curriculum for LD students: More than just textbooks and workbooks. *NATHHAN News, 4*(1), 21-22.

Sutton, J. P. (1993a, November). *How home schooling benefits special needs children.* Presentation delivered at the National Christian Home Educators Leadership Convention, Williamsburg, VA.

Sutton, J. P. (1993b). Is testing key in home school special education? *NATHHAN News*, 2(1), 6.

Sutton, J. P. (1996a, Spring). Formula for success. *The Virginia Home Educator*, 11.

Sutton, J. P. (Ed.). (1993c). *Special education: A Biblical approach.* Greenville, SC: Hidden Treasure Publications.

Sutton, J. P. (1994a). Standard curricula not enough for LD students. *NATHHAN News*, 3(1), 9.

Sutton, J. P. (1994b). Students with attention deficit disorder: Understanding and meeting their needs. *Homeschooling Today*, 3, 37-41.

Sutton, J. P. (1994c). Testing for ADD: Why it's needed, how it's done, and what to do if you can't afford it? *The Homeschool ADDvisor*, 1(3), 1-2.

Sutton, J. P. (1989). *The effects of grade level and program type on teachers' instructional behaviors in learning disabilities classrooms.* Unpublished doctoral dissertation, The University of Virginia, Charlottesville, VA.

Sutton, J. P. (1990). The forgotten sheep: Ministering to handicapped individuals. *Voice of the Alumni*, 64(6), 7, 22-23.

Sutton, J. P. (1996b). Two peas in the same pod? A careful look at AD/HD and LD. *Homeschool ADDvisor*, 2(4), 1, 5-7.

Sutton, J. P. (1994d). When is a learning problem a learning disability? *The Teaching Home*, 12(4), 44.

Sutton, J. P., Everett, E. G., & Sutton, C. J. (1993). Special education in Christian/fundamentalist schools: A commitment to all the children? *Journal of Research on Christian Education*, 2(1), 65-79.

Sutton, J. P., McKinney, J. D., & Hallahan, D. P. (1992). Effects of grade level and educational setting on behaviors of beginning learning disabilities teachers. *Learning Disabilities Research and Practice*, 7, 16-24.

Sutton, J. P., & Sutton, C. J. (1994). A 'recorded' solution for special students. *Journal for Christian Educators*, 11(5), 7-8.

Sutton, J. P., Wayne, J., Lanier, L., & Salars, K. (1993, November). *Home schooling special needs children.* Panel discussion delivered at the National Christian Home Educators Leadership Convention, Williamsburg, VA.

Swanson, J. M., McBurnett, K., Wigal, T., Pfiffner, J. J., Lerner, M. A., Williams, L., Christian, D. L., Tamm, L., Willicutt, E., Crowley, K., Clevenger, W., Khouzam, N., Woo, C., Crinella, F. M., & Fisher, F. D. (1993). Effect of stimulant medication on children with attention deficit disorder. A 'review of reviews.' *Exceptional Children*, 60, 154-162.

Taylor, W. L. (1953). Cloze procedure: A new tool for measuring reliability. *Journalism Quarterly, 30,* 415-433.

The Hands-On Equations Learning System. [Brochure.] (no date). Allentown, PA: Borenson and Associates.

Thorndike, R. L., Hagen, E., & Sattler, J. (1985). *Stanford-Binet Intelligence Scale.* Chicago, IL: Riverside.

U.S. Department of Education. (1986). *To assure the free appropriate public education for all handicapped children. Eighth annual report to Congress on implementation of the Education of the Handicapped Act, Volume 1.* Washington, DC: Government Printing Office.

U.S. Department of Education. (1991, September 16). *Clarification of policy to address the needs of children with attention deficit disorders within general and/or special education.* Memorandum to the Chief State School Officers from the United States Department of Education, Office of Special Education and Rehabilitative Services, Washington, DC.

U.S. Department of Education. (1992). *Fourteenth annual report to Congress on the implementation of Individuals with Disabilities Education Act.* Washington, DC: Author.

Van Houten, R. (1980). *How to use reprimands.* Austin, TX: Pro-Ed.

Vaughn, J. C. (1993a). God's mandate for special education. In J. P. Sutton (Ed.), *Special education: A Biblical approach* (pp. 15-45). Greenville, SC: Hidden Treasure Publications.

Vaughn, J. C. (1993b). Orientation for parents and teachers. In J. P. Sutton (Ed.), *Special education: A Biblical approach* (pp. 47-81). Greenville, SC: Hidden Treasure Publications.

Vergason, G. A. (1990). *Dictionary of Special Education and Rehabilitation* (3rd Ed.). Denver, CO: Love.

Wallace, G., Cohen, S. B., & Polloway, E. A. (1987). *Language arts: Teaching exceptional students.* Austin, TX: Pro-Ed.

White, P. (1994). Demystifying attention deficit disorders. *The Teaching Home, 12*(4), 46.

Wiederholt, L., & Bryant, B. (1992). *Gray Oral Reading Test-3.* Austin, TX: Pro-Ed.

Wilkinson, G. (1993). *Wide Range Achievement Test-3.* Wilmington, DE: Jastak Associates.

Williams, P. (1988). *A glossary of special education.* Milton Keynes, PA: Open University Press.

Wolf, J. S. (1994). The gifted and talented. In N. G. Haring, L. McCormick, & T. G. Haring (Eds.), *Exceptional children and youth* (6th ed.) (pp. 456-500). New York, NY: Merrill.

Wong, B. Y. L. (1986). A cognitive approach to teaching spelling. *Exceptional Children, 53*, 169-173.

Woodcock, R. W., & Johnson, M. B. (1989a). *Woodcock-Johnson Psycho-educational Battery Revised-Tests of Achievement.* Allen, TX: DLM.

Woodcock, R. W., & Johnson, M. B. (1989b). *Woodcock-Johnson Psycho-educational Battery Revised-Tests of Cognitive Abilities.* Allen, TX: DLM.

Zacherman, J. (1982). Administration of a resource program. In J. H. Cohen (Ed.), *Handbook of resource room teaching* (pp. 253-273). Rockville, MD: Aspen.

Zimmerman, B. (1982). Developing an elementary school resource program. In J. H. Cohen (Ed.), *Handbook of resource room teaching* (pp. 115-138). Rockville, MD: Aspen.

Scripture Index

Author Index

The Gift of Dyslexia
by Ronald D. Davis c̄
Eldon M. Braun
Recommended by Debbie Gerling

Subject Index

About the Authors

Dr. Joe P. Sutton

A veteran educator of 19 years, Dr. Sutton completed his doctorate (Ph.D.) in special education from The University of Virginia in 1989. He also holds master's degrees in learning disabilities and educational administration as well as a bachelor's degree in mathematics education. As a certified educational diagnostician and president of Exceptional Diagnostics, he has tested and evaluated hundreds of struggling and gifted learners since 1992. Dr. Sutton is a frequent speaker at home school conferences and has presented nationally at annual meetings of the Council for Exceptional Children, the American Educational Research Association, the Association for Teacher Educators, and the National Center for Home Education. In addition to serving as consultant to and expert witness for the Home School Legal Defense Association, he has authored more than 30 articles in leading education journals and periodicals. A 1995 appointee to the South Carolina Advisory Council on the Education of Individuals with Disabilities, Dr. Sutton has been recognized in recent editions of Who's Who Among America's Teachers and Who's Who in American Education. During the fall and spring semesters, he serves as associate professor and chairman of the Department of Special Education at Bob Jones University. Dr. Sutton currently resides in Simpsonville, SC with his wife, Connie and their three school-age sons, Jeremy, Jason, and Jared.

Connie J. Sutton

After completing a bachelor's degree in English education from Bob Jones University in 1978, Mrs. Sutton taught for several years in Christian schools in North Carolina. She began teaching special education at a school for juvenile delinquent boys in 1984 and gained additional experience as a special education teacher of high school emotional-behavior disordered students in Virginia from 1987 to 1989. Upon completion of her master's degree in special education from East Carolina University in 1989, she accepted a position as assistant professor in the Department of Special Education at Bob Jones University, where she has remained for the last eight years.